Understanding
the
Americans

D0813983

Also by Yale Richmond

Practicing Public Diplomacy: A Cold War Odyssey

Cultural Exchange and the Cold War: Raising the Iron Curtain

From Nyet to Da: Understanding the Russians

From Da to Yes: Understanding the East Europeans

Into Africa: Intercultural Insights (with Phyllis Gestrin)

Soviet-American Cultural Exchanges: Ripoff or Payoff?

Hosting Soviet Visitors: A Handbook

Understanding
the
Americans

A Handbook for Visitors to the United States

Yale Richmond

Hippocrene Books, Inc.
New York

For information, address:
HIPPOCRENE BOOKS, INC.
171 Madison Avenue
New York, NY 10016
www.hippocrenebooks.com

Cover image: Statue of Liberty (inscription on page 103)

Library of Congress Cataloging-in-Publication Data

Richmond, Yale.
 Understanding the Americans : a handbook for visitors to the
 United States / by Yale Richmond.
     p. cm.
 Includes bibliographical references.
 ISBN 978-0-7818-1219-1 (alk. paper)
1. National characteristics, American. 2. United
States--Civilization--21st century. 3. Visitors, Foreign--United
States. I. Title.
E169.12.R495 2009
973--dc22
                              2009001022

Printed in the United States of America.

I returned from that journey embarrassed by my own ignorance. I realized then what seems obvious now; another culture would not reveal its mysteries to me at a mere wave of my hand. One has to prepare oneself thoroughly for each such encounter.

— Ryszard Kapuściński, "The Open World"

CONTENTS

A Stranger on the Road

A stranger in a strange land
what he can count on is warm-heartedness.

Pardon me, do you know where Dan's Farm is?
Sure, follow us. We'll lead you to it.
Throwing the football to his wife and
putting his boys into the pick-up,
he strode along the gravel road.
You've got visitors, Dan. The boys hollered.
Submerging the thanks with loud good-byes,
they left on their four-mile return trip.

A stranger in a strange land
what he can count on is trust.

Excuse me, would you tell me how to get to …
… Sure, come here, … see that traffic light?
Just turn right into it.
Turn right?
Right.
Beep! Beep! … You idiot, can't you read?
No right turn …

A stranger in a strange land
What he can count on is courage.

Stop! Stop! Police! Police!
How? How? Where? Where?
Officer … I'm sorry … I didn't look at …
You didn't speed. You were zigzagging. May I see …
Sure …
I don't need your wallet. Just take out the
  driver's license please. Have you had a drink?
Yes. Back at Strong City I had a Coke and she had a …
No, I had a Coke. The one you had was called Pepsi.

—Sue Hu, *Ours: poetry in words and brush strokes*
[Sue Hu is an artist and poet who resides in California.]

ACKNOWLEDGMENTS

Many people have contributed toward this book. Among them are Louise Berenson, Osa Coffey, Mamadou Darboe, Elisabeth Derow, Raymond Fink, Ciro Franco, Phyllis Gestrin, Ophra and Roland von Hentig, Sue and K.K. Hu, Leon Leiberg, Margaret and Stephen McLaughlin, Donald Miller, Nancy Miller, Sherry Mueller, Hania Richmond, Catherine Salz, Frantisek and Larisa Silnicky, Samuel Stoleru, Jocelyne Taillard and Robert Nitsch, Christa Veenstra, Lynn Visson, Bert van Wesel, and last but most certainly not least, the Program Officers at Meridian International Center, Washington D.C., Jeanne Welsh for her word processing know-how, and my editors at Hippocrene Books, Priti Chitnis Gress and Michael Scott Carroll.

PREFACE

You are planning a trip to the United States—for business or to work, study, or merely travel. You have your U.S. visa in hand, have practiced your English, and packed your bags. But how much do you really know about the people you will be meeting in the United States, how they behave, and how their behavior differs from what you may be accustomed to in your home country? As our world grows smaller and we travel abroad more, our need for mutual understanding increases.

To be sure, you have seen lots of Hollywood films, but do they accurately portray the culture of a vast country of more than 300 million people with many geographic, political, ethnic, and religious differences? If Hollywood has been your guide to America, you can expect some surprises.

This book is intended to help you understand America and the Americans, to avoid making mistakes, and to make your trip a success. It will help you to say the right things to the right people at the right time, and to use American idioms that communicate appropriately. (Such idioms and expressions are printed in bold face in the text, and listed in a glossary at the end of the book.)

These observations are based primarily on interviews with newly arrived visitors to the United States, as well as my own many years of living and working abroad in five countries as a cultural officer in the U.S. Foreign Service, visiting many more nations, and trying to help others to understand the United States, its people, and its politics. And although I was a government employee for thirty-five years, the views expressed here are my own.

Bon voyage, and may your visit be fruitful and pleasant.

Yale Richmond
Washington, D.C.

MANY AMERICAS

There are, indeed, many Americas in America.
— Mikhail Iossel, *Russian Writers View the United States*

There is no typical American, just as there is no typical African, Chinese, European, Indian, or Latino. Yet we all have certain characteristics that unfailingly define us as nations.

All of us have been influenced in some ways by where we grew up—the geography, climate, history, and religion—that cause us to behave in certain ways and unmistakably identify us as a nation. Other important factors in our character are how we were brought up as children and the way we were educated in our schools.

The United States of America is a nation of immigrants from many parts of the world, people who left their homes in the "**Old Country**" to seek a better life in the New World, as well as the many who came here involuntarily in servitude until 1865.

In the past, most of our immigration came from Europe. The first European settlers were mostly from England of Anglo-Protestant ethnicity which, with some modifications, is still the dominant element in American culture today. The English were followed by Scots-Irish in the late 1700s, Germans in the 18th and 19th centuries, Irish in the 1840s, East and South Europeans in the 1880s and early 20th century, and Asians and Hispanics in more recent years. They all helped to populate the continent, farm the virgin land, and provide labor for the industrialization that made America a world power. The first transcontinental railroad, completed in 1869, was built by Chinese workers laying tracks from west to east, and Irish immigrants, former slaves, and Civil War veterans, from east to west.

Today our new citizens come mainly from Mexico, the Philippines, China, Cuba, India, Vietnam, and Russia; some 1.5 million come every year, half of them from Latin America, and one quarter from Asia, among them Pakistanis, Koreans, Bangladeshis and Afghanis. They come seeking work, but their presence helps us to better understand the world beyond our borders. As of November 2000, one of eight people living in the United States was an immigrant, for a total of 37.9 million, the highest level since the 1920s.[1] Like the immigrants who came before them, they renew our society by bringing new ideas and new vitality, as well as new restaurants where we can savor dishes from faraway lands. If you want to find a restaurant that serves food from your home country, do an Internet search or see the **Yellow Pages** (business pages) of the telephone directory in any American city. But remember, when you make a call from one telephone area to another, you must first dial a '1," then the three-digit area code, and then the seven-digit number you are calling.

Our big cities still have ethnic enclaves—for Russians, Brighton Beach in New York City; for Arab Americans, the Detroit/Dearborn area in Michigan; and in almost every American city you will find Hispanics who, in the 2000 year census, numbered 41 million, or 14 percent, of the U.S. population. Hispanics, moreover, now account for half the growth in the U.S. population, and their high birthrates portend an explosion in the number of eligible voters. In 2003 they surpassed African Americans, who number 13 percent, as the largest minority in America.

---

1. *New York Times*, 29 November 2007.

In many cities there are Chinatowns, Little Italys, and Vietnamese neighborhoods, but after the second generation in America, most of our immigrants become culturally assimilated, speak English well, and are difficult to distinguish from other Americans who have been here longer. With good reason, America has been called **"the melting pot."**

Our first national motto, *e pluribus unum*, which can be seen on our monetary coins, translates from Latin as "from many, one." Historically it referred to the integration of the thirteen original English colonies into one nation, but more recently it has come to signify the merger of many nationalities into one people.

Despite large-scale immigration, America still has vast tracts of sparsely populated land, and its population density is very low compared to other countries. Excluding Alaska, we have 34 people per square kilometer. By comparison, population density in the United Kingdom is 247 per square kilometer, 231 in Germany, and 337 in Japan. Consequently, there is a continuing debate about immigration—how many more people should we admit to meet the growing needs of industry and services—and from which parts of the world should they come?

INDIVIDUALISM

Progress will march if we hold an abiding faith in the intelligence, the initiative, the character, the courage, and the divine touch in the individual. We can safeguard these ends if we give to each individual that opportunity for which the spirit of America stands.
—Woodrow Wilson, 28th U.S. President

Some cultures emphasize the community and others the individual. Ours is indeed a culture of the individual. A study of forty countries by Dutch sociologist Geert Hofstede concludes that America, with a score of 91, has the most individualistic culture in the world, followed by Australia (90), the United Kingdom (89), the Netherlands and Canada (each with 80), and Italy (76).

Opposed to Hofstede's individualism is collectivism, not in the political sense but the degree to which individuals are integrated into groups. In the individualist column, Hofstede lists societies in which the ties between individuals are loose and everyone is expected to look after him/herself and his/her immediate family. In his collectivist column are societies in which people from birth onwards are integrated into strong, cohesive in-groups, often extended families (with uncles, aunts, and grandparents) which continue protecting them in exchange for unquestioned loyalty to the group.

The high individualism ranking for the United States indicates a society with a more individualistic attitude and relatively loose bonds with others. Americans are more self-reliant and tend to look out for themselves and their close family members.

For example, 77 percent of American commuters, despite the high price of gasoline and today's emphasis on the environment, drive to and from their workplaces alone rather than in **car pools** with their neighbors, or using public transportation.

We do belong to groups and associations. Many Americans are members of groups associated with their church or temple. Others are members of professional associations related to their work, musical groups such as amateur orchestras and choirs, **PTAs** (Parent-Teacher Associations), or are active in local politics in their communities. But our overall emphasis is on individual responsibility and independence from others. Consequently, some visitors to America, disappointed by the American emphasis on the "self," may miss the more active socializing of their home countries, connections to a community, and dependence on a close-knit circle of friends.

If we look back to farming, the occupation of most early Americans, following English tradition they lived not in little villages, as in most European countries and many other parts of the world, but on their own land, far from their neighbors, and with fences to mark the limits of their property. For most of our history, land was plentiful and often free, and was sought by immigrants from Europe who had there been denied land of their own. As you fly over farmland here, you will see many such farm houses, distant from their neighbors.

Many of our city dwellers, too, prefer to live, not in big high-rise and energy-efficient apartment buildings close to their neighbors, but in detached single-family homes, with a lawn in front, a patio in back, and a fence separating them from their neighbors. And each home has its own lawnmower, rather than sharing one with a neighbor. Such homes have become more expensive in recent years, but with easy access to mortgages, they are still an important part of the "**American dream**," about which more will be written in the following pages.

We have had a few communes—groups of people living together and sharing interests, income, and often property—in our history and we still have some, but they are considered outside mainstream society. Most Americans prefer to be independent of others, making their own decisions and taking responsibility for their own actions and their own future.

During the westward expansion period of U.S. history, when land was cheap and settlers few, people lived far from their neighbors and had to rely on themselves. Such individualism eventually became a virtue, and those who can manage by themselves and improve their own situation in life—the so-called "**self-made man**"—are admired and respected. And hence the universally admired term, at least in America: the "**rugged individualist.**"

Related to our belief in self-reliance is the assumption that a person's success or failure is due almost entirely to his or her own efforts and abilities. We reject the idea that *kismet* or *karma* (fate or destiny) determines one's future. While there is a strain of predestination in America—the usually-religious belief that only certain people will be saved, and they are determined at birth—that has been challenged by believers in free will and self-determination. We have choices to make—to choose good over evil, whom we marry, the occupations we choose, whether we travel or immigrate to America, and the thousands of other decisions we have to make in a lifetime. Moreover, the American judicial system is based on the premise that we are free to choose what we do, and to suffer the consequences of our misdeeds. As William Shakespeare wrote in his play *Julius Caesar*, "The fault, dear Brutus, is not in our stars but in ourselves."

That belief in self-determination partially explains why American social welfare programs are relatively limited compared to those of other modern nations. As a popular proverb puts it, "**God helps those who help themselves.**"

Our individualism starts in childhood, when children are encouraged to make choices, express their own opinions, and think for themselves. In our schools, students question, and even challenge, their teachers; and in our colleges and universities, there is less lecture by the learned and more discussion between professors and students. The mother of Isidor Isaac Rabi, American Nobel Laureate in physics, would ask him on his return from school each day, "Did you ask any good questions today, Isaac?" Critical thinking, including the questioning of established and accepted societal norms, is a hallmark of American society.

In literature and film, our heroes are individuals, the **self-made man**, the **lone cowboy** or sheriff who overcomes all obstacles and succeeds, or the detective, working alone, who solves a serious crime. Indeed, our heroes and heroines are often "**outsiders**" who challenge societal structures and norms in some way. In our English usage we have even replaced the word "persons" with "individuals."

As a consequence of our individualism, new arrivals in America may have to learn to speak up and promote themselves. To succeed in a competitive society, some degree of assertiveness may be needed. As American sayings put it, you have to "**Blow your own horn**," and "**Stand on your own two feet**." And if you do not succeed, you may be told "**You made your own bed, now lie in it**."

Most Americans believe that competition is good, and that it promotes excellence, efficiency, and productivity. Business executives express pride in their company's competitiveness. Promotions and rewards are won by competing with fellow employees.

Children are taught at an early age to be competitive in school, and my personal experience attests to that: My mother once attended a talk for parents given by the superintendent of schools in Boston. "If your child comes home with a 95 in a test," he said, "ask him or her if anyone got 100." I was to hear that question from my mother all throughout my school years.

EGALITARIANISM

We hold these truths to be self-evident, that all men are created equal ...
— Declaration of Independence, 4 July 1776

"All men are created equal ..." That statement from the American Declaration of Independence, adopted on July 4, 1776, enshrines the belief that all people are of equal value. It rejects the idea of a class of "betters" who have an innate right to higher status, privilege, and power (although, at the time it was written, we had slavery in some of the thirteen English colonies and were soon to embark on a lengthy war with the American Indians, whom we now belatedly call **Native Americans)**. The idea of equality is also included in the concept of civil rights which embodies a wide range of rights guaranteed to U.S. citizens by the constitution and legislation of the Congress.

Americans have no hereditary nobility with titles and no social classes with fixed limits. A person's speech, bearing, or clothing do not always allow you to determine that individual's station in life. More important is whether someone is seen as a success in whatever he or she attempts. If we do have an aristocracy, it is an aristocracy of the successful.

Following English tradition at the time, the rights to vote and to hold public office were originally granted only to men, and only to those men who possessed property and could prove residency. Moreover, the right to vote was determined, not by the federal government, but by each state. By 1870, however, when most Americans were engaged in agriculture and owned a piece of land, the majority of states had dropped the requirement for property ownership. Also in 1870, the Fifteenth Amendment to the Constitution prohibited states from discriminating against potential voters because of race or previous condition of servitude, although it took the civil rights movement of the 1950s and 1960s to enforce that amendment in all states.[2] And it was only in 1920, after ratification of the Nineteenth Amendment to the Constitution, that women were given the right to vote.

One lesson from all this is that change has come to America *gradually*. As Alexis de Tocqueville put it in his *Democracy in America*:

> Men in democracies change, alter, and replace things of secondary importance every day but are extremely careful not to tamper with things of primary importance. They like change but dread revolutions.[3]

Fairness, a corollary of egalitarianism, is an English term that does not translate well into other languages, no doubt because its origins are in England and the idea did not travel well. It implies that all persons should be treated equally and that there should be a "**level playing field**" on which individuals all have the same opportunities to compete. It also may mean, at times, "**siding with the underdog**," the one who is not favored to win because it lacks the advantages held by others. As Stewart Potter, a U.S. Supreme Court Justice, once put it, "Fairness is what justice really is." And if you lose, you are expected to "be a **good sport**," to use another sporting term, and accept your defeat.

---

2. Amendments are additions to the Constitution. To take effect they must be approved by two-thirds votes in the U.S. House of Representatives and U.S. Senate, and then ratified by three-fourths of the states.

3. Alexis de Tocqueville, *Democracy in America* (New York: Library of America, 2004).

ACCUSTOMED TO CHANGE

Born often under another sky, placed in the middle of an always moving scene, himself driven by the irresistible torrent which draws all about him, the American has no time to tie himself to anything, he grows accustomed only to change, and ends by regarding it as the natural state of man.
— Alexis de Tocqueville, *Democracy in America*

De Tocqueville, a French lawyer, social philosopher, writer, and keen observer of other countries' cultures, came to the United States in 1831 for a nine-month visit during which he traveled far and wide and interviewed more than 200 people. His two-volume account of that visit, *Democracy in America,* is often called the greatest book about America. It has become a classic in which politicians of any party can find something to quote that tells us much about contemporary America.

Since America is such a young country, change is seen by Americans as normal and desirable and is expected to bring improvements. Moreover, the future is not predestined; we can influence and change it. The new is considered better than old; the future is more important than the past, and the young have priority over the old. To describe something as "**old fashioned**" usually has a negative connotation.

Automobile manufacturers bring out new models every year. New popular songs become hits overnight and replace old-time favorites. The clothing industry constantly gives us new fashions. Food in our supermarkets comes to us newly packaged and with new brand names. New books catch the public's fancy and make the bestseller lists while the old classics go largely unread. And advertising makes us want all those new products and new ideas.

Almost anything with the appellation "new" can be assured of acceptance by the American public. The New Deal was the name given by President Franklin D. Roosevelt to the government programs the Congress enacted to bring the United States out of the Great Depression of the 1930s. New Balance is the name of a popular series of casual and athletic shoes. New Horizons is the name given by the National Aeronautics and Space Administration (NASA) in 2006 to the first in its New Frontier series of space explorations. "Neocons" ("neo" being a Latin root that means "new") is the term that describes the new conservatives who have had a significant influence in the administrations of President George W. Bush. And those neocons established a Project for the New American Century. For Americans, whatever is new is expected to bring welcome changes. And if a friend or neighbor has something "new," an American may also want to have it, a process known as "**keeping up with the Joneses**."

As Albert Einstein once told us, "To raise new questions, new possibilities, to regard old problems from a new angle, requires creative imagination and marks real advance in science."

15

A Nation on the Move

In the United States, a man carefully builds a dwelling in which to pass his declining years, and he sells it while the roof is being laid; he plants a garden and he rents it out just as he was going to taste its fruits; he clears a field and he leaves to others the care of harvesting its crops. He embraces a profession and quits it. He settles in a place from which he departs soon after so as to take his changing desires elsewhere.

— Alexis de Tocqueville, *Democracy in America*

"**Don't just stand there, do something!**" a popular saying advises. Other time-honored sayings give similar advice. "**Never put off until tomorrow what you can do today;**" "**The early bird catches the worm;**" "**He who hesitates is lost**," and "**Strike while the iron is hot.**" Such sayings reflect the American tendency to take immediate action to resolve a problem or to take advantage of an opportunity. Life is fast, competition is keen, and he who hesitates may indeed be lost, or will finish second.

Opportunities are short-lived, and action is better than inaction. "**Opportunity knocks only once**," as another saying describes it, and you must act quickly or you may never have another chance. That helps to explain why, as Tocqueville observed, Americans change jobs so often.

The average American will have three or four different

careers during his or her lifetime and work for seven employers. Americans, moreover, think nothing of moving to another city or state to find a job or to seek a better one. Few live where they were born, which helps to explain why Americans treasure their family reunions—events which bring together loved ones from far and wide. The **downside** is that many Americans do not have job security and must therefore be constantly on the move.

Thanksgiving Day was celebrated by the early American settlers in 1621 as a day of thanks for a successful harvest the year after their arrival in the New World. Today, however, many Americans celebrate the holiday by getting together with their widely dispersed families and eating too much! On that day each year, the fourth Thursday in November, it's a nation on the move as an estimated 30 million Americans travel home by car, and another 20 million by air, to feast on roast turkey with bread stuffing and cranberry sauce, gravy, sweet potatoes, and other tasty dishes. If you are in the United States during November, try to get an invitation to one of those dinners. You won't have to eat for a few days afterward.

OPTIMISM

The American, by nature, is optimistic. He is experimental, an inventor and a builder who builds best when called upon to build greatly.
—John F. Kennedy, 36th U.S. President

We are the country of tomorrow .... America remains on a voyage of discovery, a land that has never become, but is always in the act of becoming.
—Ronald Reagan, 40th U.S. President

America is a young country, little more than 200 years old and, as a consequence, Americans are an optimistic people with a "**Can do**" and "**It will work out**" attitude, a trusting nature, lack of suspicion toward others, and a high degree of self-confidence. It is the optimism of youth, with a positive outlook on life, expecting a better future for themselves and their children. According to a recent study by the Pew Research Center, 84 percent of Americans describe themselves as either "fairly happy" or "very happy."

For a nation of immigrants, the "**rags to riches**" dream has been irresistible, and often realizable. Immigrants have prospered here, and gained social acceptance and recognition in an environment that facilitates upward mobility. About one million new immigrants come to America legally each year, more than come to all other countries combined.

Some 500,000, though, also come to the United States illegally each year, and illegal immigrants now total some 11 to 12 million. Whether they should be legalized and given the opportunity for citizenship is one of the major political decisions for the U.S. Congress and the White House.

There is good reason for the optimism of Americans. They have lived for two centuries in a country protected by geography from potential rivals, and with seemingly limitless space and natural resources. For those seeking land, there was, during much of our history, always a piece of land somewhere in our west waiting to be farmed by hardworking and adventurous people. Today, their children and grandchildren continue to readily find employment in a growing economy.

We do have unemployment, but it comes with cycles of the economy, and its hardships are reduced by government programs of assistance to the unemployed.

Since its founding, America has never had a revolution, famine, or despotic ruler. With our Anglo-Saxon political traditions, order and stability are taken for granted. Two broad oceans have protected us from attack from abroad, and our wars have been fought on foreign soil, with the exception of the War of 1812 (with Great Britain) and the Civil War (1861-1865) which our southerners diplomatically call "**The War Between the States**." In that war, fought after eleven southern states seceded from the Union, three million Americans fought and more than 600,000 died.

The issue of slavery, sanctioned in the South and bitterly opposed in the North, was one of the causes of the war, but there were also other factors. The South was largely rural and agricultural with an economy based on slavery, while the North had abolished slavery and was becoming industrial with a growing population based on immigration from Europe. The nation was expanding westward, and it was divided on the issue of slavery in the new states that were joining the Union.

Although we experienced a deep economic depression in the 1930s, and recessions at other times, our economy has continued to grow, aided by technological progress, higher productivity, and expanding markets. Americans have good reason to smile in expectation of a "**happy ending**" in their own lives as well as in their motion pictures. Most Americans, even those with lower incomes, believe that they are better off than their parents and that "**the best is yet to come**."

Problems, however, we do have—crime, drugs, race relations, corruption, poverty—but we see them as challenges to overcome. Consequently, some see us as incredible optimists, always smiling, trusting other people, expecting a happy ending to whatever we start, and disappointed when we don't find that happy ending or what we call "success." As famed automaker Henry Ford once put it, "Anybody can do anything that he imagines."

Such sayings prompt others to see us as naïve. And perhaps it is naïve to believe that anybody can do anything that he or she imagines, that every problem can be solved, every difficulty overcome, that we can bring democracy to countries that have never had it, if only we try hard enough, and every dispute can be resolved, if only the two sides will sit down together, talk, reason, and compromise.

Compromise in some cultures has a negative connotation, a departure from a correct and ideal position, and even one of surrender. But "compromise" in the English language has a very positive meaning. "**Meet them halfway**," a common American saying goes, "**and make a deal**," not where one side wins and the other loses but a **"win-win"** result, where both sides win by achieving some of their major objectives. As Benjamin Franklin, one of our Founding Fathers, put it, "Both sides must part with some of their demands." Compromise is at the heart of our optimism, our politics, and our democracy. As Franklin's biographer Walter Isaacson has put it, "Compromisers may not make great heroes, but they do make democracies." Or as former U.S. Senator Alan Simpson put it in modern terms:

> In politics there are no right answers, only a continuing flow of compromises among groups, resulting in a changing, cloudy and ambiguous series of public deci-

sions where appetite and ambition compete openly with knowledge and wisdom.[4]

Because of our willingness to compromise, Americans generally avoid extremes and prefer to search for a middle position, not only in our daily lives but also in our politics. Extremists have never been successful in American politics. More important than the left or right in our political spectrum has been the center and its preference for a **"middle-of-the-road"** approach, as it is called. That willingness to compromise has given our politics a stability that has produced economic growth supported by low inflation, low interest rates, and low unemployment.

That economic growth has contributed toward an optimism that is shared by long-time residents as well as newcomers to our shores.

---

4. *Conversations with History, with Harry Kreisler,* University of California (Berkeley), 17 September 1997.

First Encounters

... a firm handshake and direct eye contact will make a quick and sincere connection.
— Stephen D. Boyd, Professor of Speech Communication

When meeting someone in America, as in most countries, there is usually a ritual greeting. You ask the other person "How are you?" and the answer is usually "Fine" unless that person is mortally ill and about to be transported to a hospital. For younger people, the greeting may be "What's up?" answered by "Not much." Men may or may not shake hands the first time they meet or when they part, and traditionally the older or more senior person extends his hand first. If you are accustomed to shaking hands in your country, by all means do so in America, but shake the hand, not the arm, and give a firm shake for a few seconds but not a **bone-cruncher**. In certain social circles, women may offer their cheek if they know a man, and a kiss will be appreciated. And among young people and in business settings, women may offer their hand, and they will shake hands if a man extends his. Young women often hug close friends when they meet.

Looking a person straight in the eyes is not considered by Americans to be brazen, as in some cultures; rather, it projects an image of confidence and resolve. That may cause difficulties for children who were raised in cultures where looking an elder straight in the eyes is considered audacious. An American teacher would likely suspect that a child who does not want to look directly at her might be hiding something. Those who speak up boldly are respected and admired. As a visitor from Myanmar (Burma) saw it, "Americans love talking, discussing, arguing, commenting, and making decisions."

By contrast, those who come from a traditional society where young people do not express their views in the presence of elders may find it uncomfortable when their American friends ask them, "And what do you think?" And it is not necessary to ask about the entire family of the people you meet. In a first encounter Americans are likely to tell you all about their own families and themselves and to ask about yours.

That may come as a surprise to Scandinavians, who are not accustomed to being asked about themselves and their families and consider such details to be private. American students in Sweden and Norway often report feeling ignored at parties when no one asks them any questions; they mistakenly assume that their hosts are not interested in getting to know them. An American who had joined a golf foursome in Stockholm was rebuffed when he tried to make conversation with his fellow golfers by telling them about himself and asking about them. Swedes and other Scandinavians, however, despite their reticence in opening up to people they hardly know, report that Americans are easy to get to know, and they don't stand on ceremony.

On meeting new acquaintances, Americans may also want to talk about such things as family, work, hobbies, weather, and even politics. And they may tell you much about their personal lives without considering you as a friend or even wanting to be your friend.

First names are often used when Americans first meet. Unlike Europeans, we do not see much difference between "friend" and "acquaintance" and English language usage does not distinguish between the two. Our friendship is more casual, less binding, and sometimes less lasting. So, what should you do when you first meet an American? Let the American take the lead in deciding whether to use a first name or the more formal Mr., Ms., or Mrs. title with the last name. Most Americans, the younger generation in particular, are accustomed to being addressed by their first names, but if you prefer a more formal form of address, as in your home country, they will not object.

The use of nicknames, a relic of Edwardian England, is also common. A nickname is not a person's real name but a name given to someone because of a physical characteristic or behavioral pattern. A man with red hair, for example, may be called "Rusty," or someone of Scottish origin, or with the first name of Scott, may be called "Scotty." Americans may shorten your name if they find it difficult to pronounce. The man who repairs my car, an African from The Gambia named Alhagi, is called "Al" for short.

Being addressed by a nickname usually indicates that you are viewed with respect and even affection. Our political leaders, for example, have adopted nicknames that have stayed with them over the years, such as Jimmy Carter and Bill Clinton. And for those who can remember them, it's still "JFK" for John F. Kennedy, and "Ike" for Dwight Eisenhower.

As shocking as it may seem to foreign visitors, Americans may signal when it is time for you to end your visit with them, and depart. **Time is money**. The French, it is said, will *demande la route* (ask for the road) when it is time to leave, but when their hosts implore them to stay a few minutes longer, they will continue to sit and talk. Finally, after the third or fourth repetition of that ritual, they will actually leave. The British, it is said, say goodbye but don't leave. Americans will often leave without saying goodbye.

Speaking American

England and America are two countries separated by a common language.

— George Bernard Shaw

What George Bernard Shaw, the noted Irish dramatist and literary critic, was implying with his witticism was that though Americans and English may use the same words, the meanings are not always the same. Americans, for example, say "hood" for the part of their car that covers the engine, but in Britain it's a "bonnet." Americans go up in "elevators," but Britons use a "lift." More important, a "bum" in American English is a tramp or vagrant but in England means buttocks. Visitors will surely appreciate the need to be careful in their choice of certain words.

Americans are also divided among themselves in regard to that common language. The "purists," as some call them, insist that we speak the English that our school teachers taught us. When I was a boy in Boston, my teachers wanted us to speak "the King's English," and we were constantly reminded that "ain't" (a contraction of "are not") ain't in the dictionary, although it is now.

Opposed to the purists are those who believe that language is a living thing that changes with time, and who accept spoken and informal usage as a part of that living language. English is an acquisitive language, and new words and expressions are continually being added. "**My ex**," for example, refers to a former wife or husband from whom the speaker is now divorced. And young people may refer to a friend as "BFF," originally an Internet abbreviation for "best friends forever."

Unlike France, which has a law that prohibits the use of English in official government publications and advertisements, America has been most receptive to words from other languages. Waves of immigrants from other shores and cultures, especially in our large cities where new immigrants tend to settle, have for years been bringing new words and expressions to American English. From the Dutch we have *boss* and *stoop;* from the Irish, *blarney, boycott,* and *lollapalooza;* from the Italians, *ghetto, pasta,* and *mafia;* from the Yiddish, *bagel, chutzpah,* and *schlep.* Today they can all be found in *The New York Times,* the American "newspaper of record," as well as in the dictionary on my desk.

When you make a telephone call you may be asked to "Press 1 to continue in English." That's because Americans who are not conversant in English may want to continue in Spanish or another language. Federal law requires multilingual materials and services, but that has provoked a counter movement to make English the national language of the United States, a measure gaining broad public support. At a time when other countries are taking steps to preserve their minority languages, America seems to be doing the opposite, despite its record of having successfully assimilated so many immigrant groups from all parts of the world, and without having an official national language.

Those who arrive in the United States with a good command of English will have a decided advantage over those who do not. The teller at my local bank relates how easy it was, on arriving in the United States from India, for him to find a job, get a driver's license, and complete all the other formalities for a new arrival. And that was certainly because he had arrived with a good command of English. That also explains why the Irish have been so successful in American politics; they arrived speaking English—which enabled them to act as intermediaries for other immigrants whose English was negligible or non-existent.

Despite the influence of television and motion pictures, regional accents persist in America today as they do in many other English-speaking countries around the world. A few years ago, when my wife and I were in Scotland, we had to drop out of a tour of Edinburgh Castle because we could not understand the English spoken by our Scottish guide. Even the BBC has changed. Once the long-time guardian of the English spoken at Oxford and Cambridge, listeners to the British broadcaster can now hear the news narrated in a variety of regional British accents.

Americans are a talkative people, and they find long silences awkward. This often results in making **"small talk"** or discussing trivia before getting to the business of the day. Introductory pleasantries, however, a prelude to **"getting down to brass tacks,"** are kept brief. Hispanics, as well as people from other cultures who are not accustomed to keeping their small talk brief, may find Americans who do so rude and discourteous.

We also have a reputation for speaking directly. We say what's on our minds, and we say it openly and honestly. You ask a question and you can expect a direct answer, usually straightforward. As the sayings go, we do not **"Beat around the bush."** Rather, we **"tell it like it is."**

When talking with Americans, you generally know where they stand on a particular issue. We are not very good at hiding our opinions, and we don't like it when others hide theirs. In response to our questions we expect clear and factual answers. Those who speak indirectly or imprecisely will be seen as concealing their views and hiding something. In some countries you have to listen for what is not said; in America you will not have to guess what is meant. Facts, numbers, and other elements of precision are used and lend authority to speakers.

When Americans talk to each other, they usually establish eye contact and keep a distance of two feet or more between themselves and their interlocutor. We find it uncomfortable to talk with someone who is standing too close, and in such situations Americans will back away. Persons who come from countries where people stand closer will have to learn to keep their distance.

Inglish iz not a self-prohnownsing langwidge. If it were, our pronunciation and spelling would be much easier. As Mark Twain wisely observed: "The trouble is not with the spelling … it is with the alphabet."

Visitors from some countries pronounce their English in a manner that may be difficult for Americans to understand. But if they don't understand you, don't take it personally. It is not a reflection of your knowledge of English or your education. And it works two ways—you may encounter regional American accents that will be difficult for you to understand. As someone (anonymous) once wrote:

> The quantity of consonants in the English language is constant. If omitted in one place, they turn up in another. When a Bostonian "pahks" his "cah" (parks his car) the lost r's migrate southwest, causing a Texan to "warsh" his car (wash his car) and invest in "erl wells" (oil wells).

Computer English is popular, especially among members of the younger generation, who carry over into written English their **shortcuts** in computer writing: asap (as soon as possible), aka (also known as), btw (by the way), and w/o (without). Numbers replace words—"2" for "to" or "too," and "4" for "for"—and letters replace words by approximating their sound—"cu" for "see you," and "qt" for "cutie." With more and more people in a hurry and communicating online on ever smaller electronic devices, our language is becoming shorter as **slang** expressions continue creep into accepted English.

And don't be shocked by the common use of words and expressions, such as "pissed" (annoyed or angry) or "bullshit" (deceptive or insincere), as well as some old English four-letter words that only a few years ago were unacceptable in polite society. You will now hear them on TV, read them in our newspapers, and find them in our dictionaries.

INFORMALITY

A lot of foreigners also do not know how to deal with American informality. Most foreigners (esp. from the "third world") came from places where there is a rigid hierarchical social structure at work. One just doesn't casually saunter to the boss' office to chat. It took me a while to figure out that in American High Schools, you can answer a question from the teacher without first raising your hand and waiting to be recognized and then standing up to address the teacher. You can just slouch in your chair and shout the answer!

— Mike Spille, The Spille Blog

Informality is the rule in relationships among Americans in our non-hierarchical society. While in some other cultures such informality may be seen as showing a lack of respect toward people of higher status, in America it reflects a disdain for social ritual. Our informality is intended to put people at ease, and establish a more comfortable connection with others. Preferring informality in social and business relations, Americans believe it helps people to feel comfortable and facilitates friendly and effective communication. Formality, by contrast, is seen as indicating hierarchical status and a lack of personal warmth.

Titles, protocol, and rituals are generally regarded as unnecessary and are usually set aside. Informality also helps to explain the friendliness that most new arrivals cite as the most salient characteristic of the Americans they have encountered, and especially the help offered if the visitor is recognized as a foreigner. As one Russian put it, "If I need help, I would want to be among Americans."

Others, however, lament that American friendliness is only on the surface and does not run very deep. They warn that you can't depend on a friend to give you preferential treatment in a business or professional setting. In many cultures around the world, knowing the right person can assure success, but not always in America.

If you need help in an American city, you may find it at a local member of the Council for International Visitors (CIV), part of the network of the National Council of International Visitors (NCIV), a non-profit organization which works to bridge cultures by arranging professional meetings, cultural activities, and home hospitality in their communities for students and foreign visitors invited to the United States by the State Department and other U.S. government agencies. There are 90 such councils in cities across the United States, staffed with tens of thousands of Americans who volunteer their time and expertise in ensuring that foreign visitors have a successful stay in their communities. Many of the local councils also provide services to self-funded foreign professionals, trainees, and students; some charge for these services, others do not.

In contrast to many other countries, Americans may invite complete strangers into their homes. If you receive such an invitation, be sure to accept it. Home hospitality—an invitation to lunch or dinner in an American home—is often extended to visitors from abroad. Many Americans are interested in meeting people from other countries and cultures and exchanging views with them. And you will see how Americans live when they are *at home,* and not at their workplace.

Don't be surprised if you are invited to a **"potluck"** dinner where each guest will bring something he or she has bought or made for everyone to eat. If you are invited to such a dinner, ask if you can bring something. Visitors from countries where it is customary to decline the first invitation to eat should be warned. If you decline the first invitation, you may not be asked a second time, and you could go hungry.

In some American homes, people take off their shoes and put on slippers; in others not. As a visitor, it's a courtesy for you to ask the host or hostess if you should remove your shoes.

Speech, dress, and posture are also informal. We say "Hello" or "Hi" to strangers on the street. We use first names after just having met someone. Men work at their office desks without jackets or neckties, and tilt their chairs back when talking.

Our informality, however, can lead to misinterpreting what we say. You will often hear an American say **"Let's get together some time"** or **"Drop by some time."** Such informal expressions, however, should *not* be seen as firm invitations unless a date and time are specified.

Our clothing after working hours also tends to be casual. Americans these days go to the theater or attend concerts in informal attire. For men, neckties are no longer required in the evening, nor a dark suit and black shoes after 6 PM. When in doubt, however, for men, ask what would be appropriate to wear.

Blue jeans, the best known article of American clothing, were originally invented by tailor Jacob Davis who, together with Levi Strauss, patented them in 1873 as durable trousers for gold miners in California. Strauss had placed an order for canvas sail cloth with a factory in Nimes, France, but when the cloth arrived *de Nimes* (from Nimes) it was blue rather than white. Not to worry, the popularity of blue denim jeans spread among workers of all kinds in the late 19th and early 20th centuries, especially among cowboys, farmers, loggers, and railroad workers. During the 1950s, famous actors such as Marlon Brando and James Dean made blue jeans fashionable by wearing them in motion pictures, and jeans became part of the image of teenage rebellion. That fashion statement got a boost in the 1960s and 1970s when Levis became a fundamental part of the youth culture. And women like the way they look in them.

American informality in dress is such a basic element of American culture that many workplaces have adopted the idea of "**casual Friday**," a day when employees are encouraged to "**dress down**" from their usual professional attire. For many high-tech industries located along the Pacific Coast, as well as among faculty at colleges and universities nationwide, the emphasis on casual attire is now a daily occurrence and not reserved for Fridays. To get an idea of what attire is appropriate, watch the interviews on TV newscasts and see what people are wearing. And don't be surprised when you see women traveling to work wearing sneakers. They will usually change them for more formal shoes once they have arrived at their offices.

PRAGMATISM

The pragmatic method ... is to try to interpret each notion by tracing its respective practical consequences. What difference would it practically make to anyone if this notion rather than that notion were true?
—William James, American Philosopher

Pragmatism, the most American of all philosophies, is the foundation of the American **"results driven"** approach to planning. Someone who is pragmatic is guided by practical experience and observation rather than theory. He or she can also be described as **"hardheaded"** and "practical": someone who "gets things done."

Those comments epitomize the American approach to getting things done. It is exemplified in a number of popular sayings: **"I don't care how you get it done – just do it!"** **"There are many ways to skin a cat."** **"The proof of the pudding is in the eating."** Such sayings illustrate a pragmatic approach to problem solving. Will it work? Is it useful? Americans tend to value whatever solution works, regardless of its theoretical or philosophical implications. Outcome matters more than method. As a result, people who are practical, resourceful, and inventive are admired and rewarded.

A Russian who traveled around the United States with an American friend was silent during the first two days of their trip, but then he said: "Now I understand the United States: It works."[5] Readers who have been to the old Soviet Union will understand what that Russian meant. In the USSR, things did not always "work."

Visitors to the United States from other countries marvel at how smoothly the public and private sectors run, at how things get done expeditiously—without any hassle or delay, and without having to pay a bribe or **"grease someone's palm"**—at how conflicts are smoothed over, differences between people are minimized, and efforts are made to see that they do not play too much of a role in staff work. When Americans do encounter a problem, their most common reaction is "What can we do about it?"

A corollary to the American pragmatic and optimistic outlook is that every problem has a solution. This often takes the form of negotiation, in business, law, and diplomacy, as well as every-day life. Two parties enter into a negotiation process in order to find a compromise to which they can both agree. Before taking a new job, the terms of employment, as well as the salary, will have to be negotiated. Prior to marriage, there is often a **"pre-nup"** agreement specifying which assets will remain the property of the future wife or husband. And if the marriage should fail—as some 50 percent of them do—a financial settlement is usually negotiated.

Seeking results, Americans do not engage in negotiation for the sake of process, or in talk for the sake of conversation. Such an approach differs from that of some cultures which use the negotiating process to build relationships and get to know their interlocutors, but not to attain specific goals.

Reconciliation—making opposing things compatible—is an English term that often does not have a precise equivalent in other languages. Regarded as the optimum outcome of the negotiation process: it is the ultimate win-win solution where both sides gain something they want. Striving for reconciliation can often give the necessary impetus for the solution to a pressing problem.

---

5. See Yale Richmond, *Cultural Exchange and the Cold War: Raising the Iron Curtain* (University Park, PA: Pennsylvania State University Press, 2003), 182.

During the late-nineteenth and twentieth centuries, the evolution of techniques to manage clashes between labor and management had a substantial influence on the study of international conflict management and the practice of U.S. diplomacy. The language of industrial relations is designed to professionalize and take the animosity out of industrial disputes—indeed, the very word "dispute," with its connotations of limited and resolvable disagreements, is often employed instead of the word "conflict" which suggests a more violent and less tractable quarrel. It is no coincidence that such distinguished American diplomats as Cyrus Vance and George Shultz learned their craft in labor disputes.

Nor is it a coincidence that so many members of the U.S. Congress are lawyers by training. It is because the American legal profession values dispassionate analysis, precise wording, and watertight agreements, so does American legislation, which is usually the result of lengthy negotiations and concessions leading to compromise. Moreover, the Anglo-Saxon tradition of case law, with its emphasis on inductive reasoning and pragmatism rather than on deductive reasoning and abstract principles, is likewise in harmony with the typical approach of U.S. practitioners.

The aim is to convince the other side, not of the logical rigor or philosophical integrity of their position, but of its practical, concrete advantages for both parties. The benefits of reaching agreement are emphasized, as are the costs of failing to do so. In most negotiations, both sides start out with their maximum positions—what they would ideally like to achieve. But as the negotiation progresses, each side makes concessions, usually in response to suggestions from the other side.

Barter is basic—one side gives something in response to something the other side has given. Haggling over prices, however, is not acceptable, and in American retail stores it is unheard of, unless the proprietor is from a part of the world where barter and haggling over prices is a way of life.

One exception in America to the no-bargaining rule is buying a car, new or used. If you pay the car's list price, commonly called the "**sticker price**," and do not bargain, you will be seen as a simpleton. Other exceptions are high priced electronics and other "**big ticket**" items where you can pay the sticker price but bargain your way into receiving something in addition, but gratis.

If you don't like to bargain, especially on matters of high financial value, or that might end up in a court of law, you may want to hire a lawyer to bargain for you. But remember that lawyers usually charge by the hour, and their clocks will be ticking whenever they work for you.

Big Is Beautiful

I take space to be the central fact to man born in America....
— Charles Olson, *Call Me Ishmael*

What impresses most first-time visitors to the United States is the size of the country and almost everything in it. Big is everywhere.

America is indeed a big country, the second largest in territory after Russia, and Americans, like Russians, think big. Our population is steadily increasing year to year and is now more than 300 million. From the East Coast of the United States to the West Coast, a non-stop flight can take nearly five hours. By rail it can take three days, with several train changes. **"Hitchhiking"** across the country, which I did when I was discharged from the army in California, takes five days. California, one of our largest states, now has the fifth largest economy in the world. Visitors from smaller countries are usually surprised by the vastness of America and its fascination with size.

Our Sport Utility Vehicles (SUVs) are monstrous but popular, despite the amount of fuel they consume, which gives rise to the expression **"gas guzzlers."** Our hamburgers have a lot of fat but Americans like them bigger and better; McDonald's sells a "Big 'n Tasty" with cheese that weighs 8.7 ounces (247 grams) and contains 520 calories. Many Americans, however, now aware that obesity is not good for their health, are show-ing some discipline in their diets. **McMansions,** a new phe-nomenon, have come to the real estate market—huge homes constructed on small plots of land amid much smaller houses. "**Big Apple**" is the nickname for our largest city, New York. And "Big Bands" are what Americans danced to in the 1930s.

A church in the Washington, D.C. area named "Jericho City of Praise," with a membership of 19,000, is one of the largest in America. It is located only a few steps from the FedEx foot-ball stadium of the Washington Redskins football team that seats 91,000. The church, no longer called a megachurch, is now designated as a gigachurch, one with a congregation of more than 10,000 worshipers.

And because we are such a big country, Americans think big and talk big. Texas, the second largest of our states after Alaska, has a reputation of being "**larger than life**," and Tex-ans like to do things in a big way. Its tourism slogan is "Texas: it's like a whole other country." And it truly is.

Because of our vast size, we also have numerous natural ca-tastrophes in our many geographic regions – hurricanes, floods, droughts, tornados, wildfires, extreme heat and extreme cold. Weather can be unpredictable, and variable, in many parts of the country. As Mark Twain put it, "If you don't like the weather in New England, just wait a few minutes." So be warned, and dress accordingly. Despite our size, we still have seasons, although in our southern states there is not as much seasonal change in weather as in the north. But one Indone-sian was puzzled when he first arrived in Washington, D.C. in February and noticed that all the trees had no leaves. He won-dered what had killed them, and it was only months later that he learned about our four seasons.

And if numbers impress you, our national budget for Fiscal Year 2007 was 2.7 trillion dollars, not including military ex-penditures for the costs of wars in Iraq and Afghanistan; and our national debt, as of this writing, was 8.89 trillion dollars.

How to explain this American fascination with size? Own-ers of big cars explain it by the size of the country and the long distances people must drive, on vacations to visit family or merely to commute from home to workplace in the morning. Yes, on long distances big cars are much more comfortable, especially when you have several children in the back seat or with a dog in the "way back" in a van or station wagon.

Big houses are more difficult to explain, but they are related to American individualism and the idea that each child in a family should have his or her own bedroom, a departure from the time, only a few generations ago, when all the children slept in one room. Big houses are also a sign of "**keeping up with the Joneses**" and the convenience of having two or more bathrooms, a guest room, a formal dining room, and a family room. When all things are considered, it is clear that Americans are impressed with size, and big is beautiful.

Making Friends

Be slow in choosing a friend, slower still in changing.
— Ben Franklin

In the latter part of the 18th century, Benjamin Franklin was the best-known and most popular American both at home and abroad. Author, inventor, diplomat, musician, philosopher, newspaperman, and journalist, he has been called "the first American" and the first "**self-made man**." Many of his witty and wise sayings are from his *Poor Richard's Almanack*, an annual publication that is still in print today. Another of his popular sayings is "A brother may not be a friend, but a friend will always be a brother."

America can be a cold and unwelcome place for visitors from other countries who do not have friends to greet them on arrival. An African friend from The Gambia told me how surprised he was to see a sign at JFK airport in New York: "Do not entrust your luggage to strangers." In his own country he knew all his neighbors, trusted them, and it was inconceivable that anyone would steal his luggage.

Another immigrant, this one from Sudan, says that on arriving at JFK he was very fearful lest he be assaulted or robbed because of all the American movies he had seen involving violence and criminal actions. However, after a few months here he learned that, as he put it, "99.5 percent of Americans are good people."

Americans smile easily and are easy to talk with. A visitor from Asia described the United States as a country of "smiley people." But those smiles do not indicate an automatic commitment to friendship. In our mobile and fast-moving society where we are taught to be self-reliant, friendships are often transitory and established only to meet personal needs at a certain time and place. Many Americans have friends at work or at school but only a few very close friends. True friendships are usually the result of repeated interactions between individuals of the same age group, gender, and socio-economic level, and who share similar views and a variety of experiences.

Casual friendships are especially common among college-age students who, separated from their parents for the first time, are trying to establish personal independence and are encountering a variety of people representing different values and lifestyles. A French exchange student reports that during student orientation week at an American university he made a hundred friends, and the next week lost ninety-nine of them.

That is not meant to discourage international students from attempting to establish friendships with Americans. Most Americans readily accept new people into their social groups. Some of the best ways to meet Americans are to attend religion-sponsored activities, join a special interest group, or visit Americans in their homes. But don't "**drop in**" without calling in advance. Such an action would be seen as an invasion of a person's privacy and a failure to plan ahead. Colleges and universities have a wide range of **extracurricular activities** to satisfy almost every interest, as well as social events like dances and performances.

And there will be plenty of bars to visit. An American bar is much like an English pub, a place to meet people and socialize over a beer or something stronger. And if you don't drink alcoholic beverages, as they are called, bars usually will also offer non-alcoholic drinks.

Privacy Preferred

Privacy is the right to be alone—the most comprehensive of rights, and the right most valued by civilized man.
— Louis D. Brandeis, U.S. Supreme Court Justice

Protection of individuals and their "right to privacy" epitomized the judicial decisions of Louis D. Brandeis, appointed to the U.S. Supreme Court by President Woodrow Wilson in 1916, and the first Jew to be named to the highest court in the land.

That right to privacy has been affirmed by subsequent justices and judges, most recently by Justice Samuel A. Alito Jr., in his confirmation hearing in the U.S. Senate on January 11, 2006, following his nomination to be a Justice of the Supreme Court, when he stated, "People have a right to privacy in their homes, and in their papers and in their persons."

"**Privacy**" is a word that does not translate well into other languages. In a recent judicial decision, the right of privacy has been defined as "the right to be left alone without unwarranted intrusion by government, media, or other institutions or individuals."[6] Although a consensus supporting the right to privacy has emerged—all recently confirmed justices to the Supreme Court have also affirmed their belief in the right to

---

6. Columbia University Electronic Encyclopedia, Sixth Edition (Columbia University Press, 2000).

privacy—the extent of the right and its basis in constitutional law remain hotly contested. It was not until the Supreme Court decision in *Griswold v. Connecticut* (1965), which voided a state statute preventing the use of contraceptives, that the modern judicial doctrine of privacy emerged. The right to sexual privacy as set forth in the Griswold case was one of the main foundations of the Supreme Court's subsequent decision in *Roe v. Wade* (1973) to overturn state anti-abortion statutes and to reaffirm that the state has no right to intervene in the private affairs of people.

"Privacy" has become a very political issue in contemporary America, but the concept extends far beyond the judicial sense. In much of Europe and Asia, the concept of personal space is virtually non-existent. We Americans have our own space, and we don't want others to invade it. We don't stand close to people when talking with them. Queuing up in line in an orderly manner is something Americans (and Brits) do, and expect others to do. We don't touch others, unless of course the other person wants to be touched. And in crowds, we do not push or elbow our way forward. So when foreigners come to the United States they may inadvertently offend people by standing too close to them in a line or elsewhere.

A visitor from Russia was puzzled when so many people he encountered on the streets of Washington would say "**Excuse me**" to him. He later learned that he was bumping into people in his rush to get from one place to another, something that he was accustomed to do in his home country, but without pausing to apologize, and the "excuse mes" he was hearing were sarcastic references to what *he* should have been saying.

Another visitor, from Cuba, wondered why American residential neighborhoods are so quiet, with so few people on the streets. Where are all the people, he asked? In his home country people literally lived on the streets, and your doings were known to all your neighbors. But in America, he learned, many women work, married as well as single, and those who stay at home are likely to be watching television or browsing the Internet.

Privacy also includes respect for other people's personal affairs. We do not ask questions about a person's religion or how much money he or she earns. Medical records are private, and accessibility to them is strictly controlled. We even have parts of our body that we call "private parts," although in today's television and theater they are no longer so private.

Our inner feelings are also private. Like the British, Americans are brought up to maintain a "**stiff upper lip**," which in practical terms means not to flaunt your feelings or show others how you feel, especially when something bad happens to you. Don't shout, don't wave your arms, don't make a scene, we are taught, and if you are a man, don't cry. But as George Santayana, a Harvard University professor of philosophy, saw it: "The young man who has not wept is a savage, and the old man who will not laugh is a fool."

When we suffer, we don't show it to others. And because we don't show our emotions, some people find us cold, distant, and difficult to get to know. In such cases we become the inscrutable Americans, whose inner thoughts and feelings are impossible to fathom. This helps to explain why Americans, so often in public, wear a smile and appear to be cheerful.

Nevertheless, there are times when Americans, like many other people, do "explode." One such instance, usually in heavy traffic and called "**road rage**," occurs when drivers become very annoyed at how others are driving and fly into a rage. It's best to make a hasty departure and not argue with them.

THE WORK ETHIC

*Genius is one percent inspiration and ninety-nine percent
perspiration.*
—Thomas A. Edison, American inventor

Americans show great respect for "perspirers"—people who are hard workers and high achievers. Many years ago, that was called the "**Protestant work ethic**." In America, however, it has become the Protestant, Catholic, Jewish, Muslim, Hindu, Buddhist, and agnostic work ethic. We have all become hard workers.

Children are encouraged at an early age to perform some kind of work for pay. Home delivery of newspapers was once a traditional way for a boy to start earning money. At the age of thirteen I had my first job, delivering newspapers to 100 homes in Boston, seven days a week, for the grand sum of $2.50 a week. My inspiration for hard work leading to riches and success was Horatio Alger, a popular mid-nineteenth century author who wrote more than 130 novels for boys with titles such as *Try and Trust, Do and Dare, Strive and Succeed, Work and Win.* Alger's bestsellers were rags to riches stories telling how poor boys could achieve the American dream of wealth and success through hard work, courage, determination, and concern for others.

"Keep your nose to the grindstone and your shoulder to the wheel," advises an old Alger-like proverb, and Americans today follow that advice by spending an average of 1,900 hours a year at work, according to the U.S. Census Bureau. That is twenty more days each year than a quarter century ago, and more than the number of days spent at work in any other industrialized nation in the world. American workers also have fewer vacation days and less sick leave than workers in most other countries. Typically, when one begins a new job, it comes with ten vacation days a year and five for sick leave. AVIS, the car rental company, bases its commercial slogan "We try harder!" on its strong work values.

"One of the delicious ironies of history," writes American historian Darrin M. McMahon, is that "Marx's contention that not only should we enjoy the fruits of our labor, but labor itself should be our fruit, is today a central tenet of the capitalist creed."[7] But those fruits do not come so easily. An American citizen who emigrated from Ethiopia told me that what impressed him most about America was the good life he had heard about before coming here, but he did not know how hard he would have to work to realize it. Because of that strong work ethic and the drive for "**getting ahead**," we are often accused of not knowing how to relax and enjoy life.

The strong commitment to work, however, has not affected how long Americans live, and longevity in the United States continues to rise. An American male born in 2006 can expect to live 75 years, and a female, 80 years.

So which is the stronger sex?

---

7. Darrin M. McMahon, *Happiness: A History* (New York: Atlantic Monthly Press, 2006).

TIME IS MONEY

A stitch in time saves nine ... Time lost is never regained.
— Ben Franklin

Why are Americans always in such a hurry? That is a question foreign visitors often ask, especially in our big cities where everyone seems to be rushing somewhere, with no time for extended conversations or leisure activities. What foreign visitors apparently don't seem to realize is that rushing is becoming a worldwide phenomenon, and the bigger the city—in any country—the more rushing there will be.

Time is also money, and it affects our entire lives. Wasting time is as bad as wasting money, so we schedule our daily activities and work on tight schedules. We even have automated signs that tell us how many seconds remain to cross streets at stop-light intersections.

Keeping busy is very important to Americans, and wasting time is frowned upon and discouraged. Punctuality is a requirement for business and most other meetings involving a group of people, a social engagement, or a dinner invitation. For other social events, such as large informal cocktail parties or receptions, time is more flexible, and you can come and go as you wish.

Many Americans organize their activities according to a daily schedule. As a result, they always seem to be hurrying to get to their next appointment. Women may seem to be hurrying more than men, because many of them hold two jobs, one at a workplace and the other at home where they still perform household tasks and help raise the children.

Business meetings usually start on time, and everyone is expected to be there on time. In some countries there is the "academic quarter of an hour" which allows a professor to be up to fifteen minutes late for a lecture before the students can leave, but Americans are not so tolerant. Being five or ten minutes late is permissible, but for any longer delay it is customary to call and say that you will be late or cannot make a meeting.

The importance of time can be attributed, in part, to Taylorism, a system of management control of production originated in 1911 by the American mechanical engineer Frederick W. Taylor. Taylorism evolved into the system of time-and-motion study that revolutionized industrial production. Labor unions didn't like it, but Taylorism prepared the way for standardization of products, accounting techniques, and a more rational management of industry throughout the United States and eventually other industrial countries as well, including the Soviet Union. That got us accustomed to regarding time as a commodity for which someone has to pay. Accordingly, we don't like to waste time, our own or other people's time.

"If you really want to annoy an American," said Will Rogers, the American humorist, "sit down and talk as if you have nothing else to do for the rest of the day. You will be breaking the Eighth Commandment of American culture, 'Don't waste time.'"

Half our life is spent trying to find something to do with the time we have rushed through life trying to save.

Whether they believe in an afterlife or not, Americans are intent in getting the most out of their time spent on this earth.

SPORTS FOR ALL

Americans are avid sports fans. Their favorites are baseball, football, and basketball, all of them uniquely American, and played at the amateur as well as professional levels. And the latter—"pro" sports—is big business. Sports are so important in American life that sports fans can even tune in to an all-sport TV channel, ESPN, twenty-four hours every day of the year.

Our sports start with Little League Baseball and soccer for elementary school children, and continue in high (secondary) schools, where teams are fielded in the three major sports as well as in track and field, lacrosse, volleyball, wrestling, tennis, swimming, and gymnastics. And in some sports there are girls as well as boys teams. In small towns across America, high school games and competitions are major events on Friday evenings and Saturday afternoons.

Colleges and universities are the next step up the sports ladder. Outstanding players are awarded athletic scholarships to develop their athletic prowess, and receive better coaching, financial support, and keener competition. Players also compete to preserve the "honor" of their dear old **Alma Mater**. The highlight of the college basketball season, known as **March Madness,** although it usually extends into April, is when TV carries the games of teams competing for the national championship.

The final and ultimate stage is professional, which can truly be called big business. Outstanding players draw multi-million dollar salaries, and games are played in huge stadiums, where seats can sometimes sell for hundreds of dollars.

Baseball is clearly the national sport, and the President usually throws out the first ball to open the season each year. **Fans** show their loyalty by wearing caps, shirts, and jackets decorated with the name and symbols of their favorite teams. The American baseball cap, bearing "NY" for New York or "B" for Boston, can now be found all over the world. Rivalries between teams continue, year after year, as between the New York Yankees and the Boston Red Sox, although the members of each team may change from year to year.

The top-rated athletic events are the World Series in October, for major league baseball, and the Super Bowl in February, for professional football. For such events, almost everything stops as the entire country—men, women, and children—watches the events at home on television.

For the Super Bowl, waiting lines in groceries grow longer as fans stock up with potato chips, popcorn, and other snack foods for their family and invited friends. If you visit someone who has the TV tuned to such an athletic event, don't expect your host to immediately turn off the TV. Watching a key moment of play, as impolite as it may be, often has priority in an American home.

Another distinctive feature of American spectator sports is the **tailgate party**. A family, or several families together, will have a picnic in a stadium parking lot prior to a game, using the pulled down tailgate of a station wagon or truck as a table. ***Bon appétit!***

Soccer, which is called football everywhere but in the United States and Canada, has gained some popularity in recent years. This is due in part to the increasing number of Hispanics living in the U.S., and support for the World Cup by soccer's best known American fan, Henry Kissinger, former U.S. Secretary of State.

American women have also become active participants in athletics and fans of major sports teams, thanks to legislature approved by the U.S. Congress in 1972. Title IX, as it is commonly known, states: "No person in the United States shall, on the basis of sex, be excluded from participation in, be denied the benefits of, or be subjected to discrimination under any education program or activity receiving Federal assistance." That law opened opportunities for women to participate in school and college athletics that had previously been denied them. As a result of the law, women's participation in athletics has greatly increased as schools are required to finance athletic activities for women in accordance with their percentage in the school's student body.

The use of sporting metaphors is prevalent throughout American society. Americans speak of being on "**a level playing field**," being on "**the one-yard line**," "**putting the ball in the other guy's court**," and taking a "**raincheck**." With reference to baseball, you may hear "**hitting a home run**," "**out in left field**," or "**strike out**." Certain assumptions are inherent in such a vocabulary—above all that sports depend on the strict enforcement of the rules of the game.

FAST FOOD FOR FAST FOLKS

You are what you eat.
—American proverb

If we are indeed what we eat, that explains why so many Americans are too fat. Visit any fast food restaurant and see for yourself. With tasty hamburgers, fried chicken, French fries, and pizza among our favorite foods, there is just too much fat in our diet.

More and more Americans are eating out in restaurants than ever before and consuming one-third of their daily caloric intake outside the home. Restaurant servings are bigger than ever, and Europeans and others are astounded by the huge size of the portions served in our restaurants. Big portions make big people. But if you cannot consume everything on your plate, you can ask for your leftovers to be deposited in a **"doggie bag"** to be taken home, not for your dog but for yourself. And you can do that at any restaurant, no matter how expensive. Here are a few other **tips** for "**eating out**":

With many Americans having specialized eating requirements—**kosher**, **vegan**, no pork, etc.—before choosing a restaurant it is polite to ask people you will be eating with, but don't know well, whether they have any eating restrictions, or to speak up yourself if you have such a restriction. Americans typically order their food choices individually, for themselves, rather than family style for the group, but if you want to share a dish with someone, please say so. At meals with multiple courses or servings, you may be puzzled by the multitude of knives, forks, and spoons facing you, but the "**rule of thumb**" is to start with the outside utensil on each side of your plate, and work your way in as the courses change. And if your food arrives early, it is customary to wait until the others have their food before starting to eat yours. And if you plan to have a serious conversation during your lunch or dinner, try to find a restaurant that is quiet. The *Washington Post* is now rating restaurants according to their noise level, in decibels. The *Post* finds conversation "easy" at 60 to 70 decibels. For anything above that, you have to raise your voice to be heard.

As we eat more, our lifestyles have become more sedentary. Consequently, exercise—walking, jogging, and gym workouts—has become fashionable, although many Americans are exercising less and watching television more than their waistlines. Such people are called "**couch potatoes**."

As a result, two of every three Americans are overweight or obese, and the cost to the economy, in medical care and lost wages, is staggering. As one foreign visitor commented, many Americans say they are on a diet and are careful about what they eat, but they counteract their diets by eating too much.

If you are watching your waistline, you can eat sensibly, quickly, and cheaply in restaurants with a **salad bar**. There, you will see what you are getting, and you can take as much or as little as you wish since you usually pay according to the weight of what you take. Salad bars are also good places to eat for vegetarians and others with restricted diets. If you are on a special diet, look for the "Nutrition Facts" label on food that you purchase in supermarkets. The labels will tell you exactly the contents of the food items you are buying, their calories per serving, and the fat, cholesterol, sugar, sodium, fiber, and other contents.

If you are watching your budget rather than your waistline, "**all you can eat**" buffets will be tempting. In such restaurants you pay a fixed price—very low and with discounts for seniors and children—and can take as much as you want of a variety of foods, and return to the food line for additional servings as often as you wish. Such restaurants are common in suburban America.

In a society obsessed with the importance of time, long lunches and leisurely dinners are out, and siestas—or midday naps—are a thing of the past, even in our warmer climes. Ethnic foods, however, are "in," and in most cities it is easy to find Chinese, Korean, Vietnamese, Indian, Japanese, Italian, Thai, and Afghan restaurants, among others.

If you are invited to dine in a restaurant with American friends, the question may arise as to who will pay. If it is clear that you are invited as a guest, then you should not expect to have to pay (though it is always polite to offer to do so). But if you are asked to join with others for lunch or dinner, it may be prudent to ask in advance if the cost will be shared by all who attend, a practice called "**Dutch treat**" or "**going Dutch.**" Meeting someone for breakfast is also convenient for people with busy schedules. You may also be invited to a "**brunch**," a mid-morning meal that combines breakfast and lunch, usually enjoyed by Americans on the weekend.

In many countries the restaurant service charge is included in the bill, but not in America. Tipping is the unwritten rule in most restaurants, but not in fast food places. It is usually 15 percent of the bill, before the tax is added, and if you pay by credit card, the tip can be added to the customer statement that you sign. For large parties of six or more people, the restaurant may add the tip to the bill.

In more expensive restaurants you may be asked to check your outercoat, but in most American restaurants you merely drape your coat over the back of your chair or hang it yourself in a designated area. Similarly, outercoats may be checked in some theaters, but more likely they are merely draped over the back of your seat. And in theaters, we do not pay for programs nor do we tip the usher who shows us to our seats.

Many Americans have a "**sweet tooth**," as we call it, a love of sweets. This takes the form, not only of chocolates and other candies, but also highly sweetened "**soft drinks**" such as cola and other carbonated drinks that are loaded with sugar. For those who are watching their waistlines, most of those drinks now have "diet" versions.

And if you are really in a hurry, you might try one of those drive-in restaurants, where you can order and pick up your meal—and consume it—in your car. You can even get a small free package of ketchup, America's favorite condiment. Ketchup is believed to have originated in China before finding its way to England and then to America where, made with ripe tomatoes, it has become our favorite sauce for a variety of foods.

ALCOHOL, TOBACCO, AND COFFEE

*To cease smoking is the easiest thing I ever did. I ought to
know because I've done it a thousand times.*
—Mark Twain, American writer and humorist

Mark Twain, the great American humorist and world-
renowned writer and lecturer, was known for his witticisms—
which always contain an element of truth. But smoking in
America, despite Mark Twain's witticism, has indeed declined as Americans have become more aware of the health
hazards of using tobacco and inhaling smoke from other people's puffing.

In public buildings and work places, smoking is usually forbidden, and in most restaurants, it is either outlawed or restricted to certain tables. Smoking is also a **"no-no"** in trains,
buses, and airplanes. Washington, D.C., New York, and many
other American cities have enacted prohibitions against smoking in public places. However, water pipes are more accepted,
and hookah bars can occasionally be found in chic downtown
areas of major cities and close to college campuses.

As for alcoholic drinks, or "beverages" as they are eu-
phemistically called, Americans are now drinking more wine
and beer, and less **"hard liquors"** like whiskey, gin, and
vodka. Although less than one in seven American adults drinks
wine regularly, per capita consumption has been increasing

every year and has now reached a new high of 2.77 gallons per year. That may not seem high to residents of France, Italy or Spain but it is nevertheless a record high for Americans.[8]

Some Americans, however, do not drink any alcohol at all. Some have religious convictions that prohibit alcohol, and others just don't think it is right to drink. So don't be surprised if an American "**teetotaler**," as they are called, raises his or her glass of water for a toast to you.

Coffee, however, is still a major addiction of Americans, and coffee shops such as Starbucks, Peet's, Seattle's Best Coffee, Green Mountain Coffee, and The Coffee Bean have become quite popular. Many Americans drink coffee at all hours of the day. In restaurants in many parts of the country, you may be asked as soon as you are seated whether you want a cup of coffee, and when you have drunk it up, you may be offered a free refill. Nevertheless, the coffee you will find in most American restaurants or offices is a pale imitation of the drink to which Europeans and Latin Americans are accustomed. The nearest thing America has to European coffeehouses is one of the chains mentioned above, where you can enjoy a good cup of coffee, read a newspaper, or meet someone for business or conversation, and all at a reasonable price.

Water, however, is the drink of choice for most Americans, and you will see them bearing bottles from which they sip periodically. Restaurants will routinely serve you a glass of water, with ice, as soon as you are seated. If you don't like ice in your water, say so, and you will be served water at room temperature. Public water drinking fountains can be found in public buildings, parks, schools, and almost everywhere else, and the water will be clean and potable.

Most community water systems, however, add chlorine to kill bacteria, as well as fluoride—the same substance commonly found in toothpaste—to help build stronger teeth and prevent tooth decay. Europeans and others may object to the additives in American drinking water, but the treatment does

---

8. *San Francisco Chronicle,* 19 January 2006.

prevent the spread of waterborne diseases and minimizes expensive visits to the dentist. If you don't want to drink water with additives, untreated water is cheap and can be purchased at any supermarket or convenience store.

Drugs, more correctly called narcotics, are strictly regulated in America, and their possession is subject to severe punishment. And that includes everything from marijuana to cocaine. One in four prisoners in the United States is serving time for a drug law violation, and in the federal penal system, they are 55 percent of the prisoners. So be warned!

CARRIED BY CAR

Everything in life is somewhere else, and you get there in a car.
—E. B. White, American writer

To get around in America you need a car. A Brazilian woman, when asked what surprised her here in America, replied immediately, "You need a car to go anywhere." And it's not only Brazilians; 93 percent of Americans rate a car as a necessity (next comes a washing machine at 86 percent).[9]

In the suburbs of American cities, and in many cities as well, a car is almost always a necessity. Stores for shopping, a doctor's office, your church, and just about any place else that you need to go to are widely scattered and often without access to public transportation.

Why do so many Americans prefer to live in the suburbs with a long commute to their places of work in a big city? The simple answer is that land, as well as housing, is cheaper the further you go from a big city, although as the price of gasoline rises, the savings on land and housing are no longer so financially attractive. The far out suburbs also have the attractions of less crime, cleaner air, better schools, and an improved environment for raising children.

Rail service is not very good, except for the East and West

---

9. *Washington Post*, 9 January 2007.

coasts and some suburban areas around big cities. For people in a hurry, air service is very good to almost everywhere, but visitors won't see much of America from the sky, and bus service is not always convenient. So that leaves the car, which has become an economic necessity for most Americans. For those visitors from other countries who will need a car, rental service is everywhere, and as E. B. White has suggested, it will get you everywhere.

As in Europe, driving increases during the summer months, when Americans take to the roads on their summer vacations. From June through August, driving peaks at 8.6 billion miles per day, for work and leisure. Gasoline consumption also peaks, at 9.5 million barrels per day.

Like continental Europeans, Americans drive on the right side of the road, and if you come from the United Kingdom or one of the former British colonies, that may present a problem. Even if you do not drive here, it may also present a problem when crossing streets on foot. Remember to look left, not right, when you step off a curb in America.

In some cities you may be stopped by the police for "**jay-walking**"—not crossing a street at an authorized place—and fined on the spot. Among authorized places are "**zebra crossings**" painted white on the pavements—or at corners with traffic lights indicating when pedestrians may "Walk" or must "Wait."

Some signs along roads or highways may be puzzling to drivers from other countries. Among them are AVE (Avenue), BLVD (Boulevard), EXPWY (Expressway, a major divided highway with limited access and no tolls), FRWY (Freeway, similar to Expressway), H (Hospital), HAZMAT (Hazardous Material), HOV (High Occupancy Vehicles), JCT (Junction), MPH (Miles per hour), PRKING (Parking), and XING (Crossing).

Speed limits and other driving regulations are the responsibility of the fifty states and local governments to determine. They vary from state to state and may also vary within states according to the local jurisdictions of counties and cities. Watch for signs that tell you the maximum, and sometimes minimum, speeds that are allowed. And watch out for "**speed bumps**," placed in roads in residential areas to force drivers to slow down.

In some cities you may be able to make a right turn on a red light after coming to a complete halt; in others not. In some cities you may be able to make a left turn only on a green arrow pointing left. In cities, street parking may be subject to limitations; watch for signs along the street that tell you where you can park, for how long, and whether you have to put coins in a parking meter. Make sure that you have an International Driver's Permit (IDP) that is valid in the United States and insurance to cover accidents. And in the United States it is illegal to drive a vehicle that is not insured.

Beware of speed traps—places where speed limits are low, and concealed police may be waiting to catch you exceeding the limit. Speeding fines may be doubled in areas where road crews are present. Do *not* try to run through yellow traffic lights. Many new traffic signals have video cameras to copy the tag numbers of violators, and your violation notification will arrive in the mail.

And buckle up! Seat belts are mandatory in some states, and failure to use them can subject you to a fine. It doesn't take much effort, and it could save your life by preventing you from going through the windshield.

Honking your horn unnecessarily may get you in trouble with the driver of the car in front of you, and you could become a victim of "**road rage**" which can sometimes end violently. In France, you may honk your horn only if there is "an immediate danger" for other cars or pedestrians. But in America there is no such limitation; everyone seems to honk, particularly in big cities where patience is in short supply and people are in a hurry, especially during "**rush hour**" in the morning and evening commutes between home and the workplace.

Traffic in America is horrendous and is getting worse year by year. It pollutes the air, wastes our time, and consumes lots of expensive fuel. Los Angeles is America's worst city for traffic, and there it is not limited to rush hours but continues all day, from sunrise to sunset, and beyond. If you have to be somewhere by a certain time, wherever you may be, make allowances for the traffic.

As everywhere in the world, alcohol and driving do not mix, and in the United States the penalties can be severe if you fail a sobriety test that police administer at accident sites, or if you appear to be driving erratically. So if you are with a group of people attending a function where everyone is drinking, appoint a member of your group as "**Designated Driver**"—someone who will not drink and who will drive the rest of the group home. In that way you will avoid being arrested by the police for **DWI** (Driving While Intoxicated) or **DUI** (Driving Under the Influence).

If you need assistance of any sort, do not be afraid to contact the police. Though in some countries people avoid the police, American police are usually polite and prepared to provide assistance of all sorts. They do not demand bribes, and you should never offer one—that would make you immediately liable for arrest.

What to do when your car breaks down? First, American cars, especially rental cars, are very dependable and seldom break down. But if you should need the help of a mechanic, or even someone to change a flat tire, help is usually available through your insurance coverage, and will likely arrive within thirty minutes after you place a call. Make sure your auto insurance includes "**roadside assistance**."

Last, but certainly not least, prepare for driving in heavy traffic, especially in and around major cities. America's response to the rapid growth of its cities has been to build "**suburbs**" as they are called, where people who are fleeing urban poverty, decay, and crime, can sleep, eat, raise children, and mow their lawns, but without mass transportation to the cities where they work. Rather than build residential communities along rail lines to the cities, as in many other countries, America has chosen to depend on the automobile, resulting in major traffic jams during the morning and evening rush hours.

One consolation, however, is that Americans do not drive as aggressively as drivers in some other countries, and they generally observe the traffic rules and regulations.

Born to Buy

The inhabitant of the United States attaches himself to the goods of this world as if he were assured of not dying, and he rushes so precipitately to grasp those that pass within his reach that one would say he fears at each instant he will cease to live before he has enjoyed them. He grasps them all but without clutching them, and he soon allows them to escape from his hands so as to run after new enjoyments.

—Alexis de Tocqueville, *Democracy in America*

"The United States is the most consumer-oriented society in the world," writes Juliet Schor, author of *Born to Buy*.[10] In her book Schor documents how children are increasingly targeted by advertisements on television, radio, and the print media and urged to buy products they do not need.

Buying becomes a habit, and it continues to grow as children mature and become adults. The more they earn, the more they spend. As adults, they are hooked on having a home, one or more cars, a microwave, and other labor-saving appliances and entertainment equipment. Americans are constantly urged to buy and consume more and more, and their needs and wants are carefully monitored by the advertising staffs of the various

---

10. Juliet Schor, *Born to Buy: The Commercialized Child and the New Consumer Culture* (New York: Scribner, 2004).

consumer industries. As a result, the average household in America spends more than it earns; the entire country buys more than it produces; and we are living beyond our means, a situation which is not sustainable over the long run.

In 2006, Americans once more spent everything they earned, and then some, pushing the personal savings rate to the lowest level since the Great Depression more than seven decades ago. Moreover, the savings rate for all of 2006 was a negative 1 percent, meaning that not only did people spend all the money they earned but they also dipped into savings or increased their borrowing to finance purchases.[11]

When all that consumer spending is added up on the national level, America as a nation is indeed living beyond its means, spending more than it produces. And that spending gap is financed by borrowing from other countries, a development that cannot continue without dire consequences for the American economy.

The reaction of other people to American consumerism is a mixture of disapproval and envy. On the one hand, they are concerned about the worldwide impact of what they consider to be our unsustainable level of consumption and are disturbed by the unfairness of the unequal distribution of the planet's resources. On the other hand, many people, especially in the less developed countries, aspire to the high level of American material prosperity, and they become consumers after they arrive here.

Shopping malls make shopping easy, with almost everything under one roof and with the same retail outlets wherever you go. One result is the uniformity of American retail stores, with the same products everywhere. Of course, you will need a car to get to your nearest mall.

New immigrants may be tempted to succumb to America's buying binge, which is made easier by simplified access to credit cards. Be aware, though, that if you are unable to pay your credit card bill when it arrives at the end of the month,

---

11. Associated Press, 1 February 2006.

you will be charged a substantial interest rate on the amount you owe. Instead, prepare a budget, and stick to it. Resist the temptation to make purchases you do not immediately need—a BlackBerry, cable TV, a cell phone—items that were once considered a luxury but are now, for many Americans, staples of everyday life. And save, save, save.

Historically, America has always had what was considered a limitless resource base; the land, the forests and the water were so abundant that waste was not a concern and conservation not a necessity. According to a report by the World Resources Institute, the American standard of living requires 18 metric tons of natural resources per person per year, many times the world average.[12] But whatever your views, be sure to deposit your empty containers in the appropriate recycle bins, one for glass and metal, and one for paper and other products. Such receptacles can be found everywhere, and many cities mandate that the refuse they collect be appropriately sorted.

And bear in mind that the electricity in American homes is 110 volts, alternating current. If you have an electric appliance purchased in another country, you may not be able to plug it in without an adapter which can be purchased in any hardware store.

---

12. http://talesmag.com/tales/practical/ugly_american.shtml

Family

The family you come from isn't as important as the family you're going to have.

—Ring Lardner, American writer

A woman from a leading family of Laos told me many years ago how shocked she was to learn, on her first visit to the United States, that many aged Americans live in retirement or assisted living homes in their final years, rather than with their adult children. She apparently did not know that many American wives, liberated from household chores and the burdens of child raising, now work at full-time jobs, and parents in their old age do not wish to burden their children with additional responsibilities. Nevertheless, it is shocking for visitors from traditional societies to learn how we treat our "**senior citizens**," as we coyly call them.

By contrast, America is a child-oriented country. While we "**warehouse**" our elders, the attention we give our children has spawned many new industries to satisfy their wishes—clothing, toys, books, car seats, playpens. Children now also want cell phones and video games because their friends have them. Birthday parties have become extravaganzas. Parents are constantly trying to keep their children entertained, and that entertainment costs money.

Marriage has declined among all income groups, but it has declined the least among couples with higher incomes and the most education. Those couples, moreover, are older and less likely to divorce. Fewer than one in every four households is occupied by married couples with children.[13]

Eating dinner at home as a family in the evening used to be traditional in American homes, but today, with mothers and fathers both working and children busy with after-school activities, it is no longer so common, and is more like "**catch-as-catch-can**." Day care for working mothers is another industry, and many employers provide day care for employees with infants. Places for changing diapers can be found in many women's restrooms and in some men's restrooms as well. And as our children grow, we become their chauffeurs, driving them to athletic practice, dance lessons, and other after-school activities, giving rise to a new term—the "**soccer mom**."

"Soccer mom" was coined as a derogatory term, but it took on a new meaning in 1992 when Patty Murray was elected U.S. Senator from the State of Washington. Called the "soccer mom in tennis shoes," and campaigning on education, children's issues, and health care, Murray won the votes of Washington's working families and was the first woman from the state of Washington elected to the Senate, where she is now serving her third term.

But the family itself has changed, especially among lower income households. With the high divorce rate, many mothers, as well as fathers, are at work, absent from the home, and have been replaced by "**baby sitters**," grandmothers or "aunties."

That there are poor families in the United States, living below the "poverty line" set by the government, is beyond question. How the poverty line is set can be questioned, but not the need to do something about it. And that is seen as one of the tasks of modern schooling.

Some visitors from other cultures may find strange the American fascination with pets. There are an estimated 164 million dogs and cats in American homes, and they are considered part of the family. They provide companionship, sociability, and love. Dogs, moreover, follow instructions, and they don't question what we ask them to do.

EDUCATION

Public schools were designed as the great equalizers of our society—the place where all children could have access to educational opportunities to make something of themselves in adulthood.

— Janet Napolitano, Governor, State of Arizona

Compulsory schooling has a long history in America. In 1642, Massachusetts, still a colony of England, passed a law requiring that parents and masters of children apprenticed to them were responsible for their basic education and literacy. All children, as well as servants, were to be able to demonstrate competence in reading and writing. There was no idea yet of a formal school, but five years later, in 1647, another law required towns of at least fifty families to hire a schoolmaster to teach children to read and write. Towns of 100 families were to have a grammar schoolmaster who could prepare children to attend Harvard College. Today's Harvard was founded in 1636, only sixteen years after the arrival of the first settlers in the Massachusetts Bay Colony, which was later to become the state of Massachusetts. By comparison, it was not until 1870 that public education was instituted in England with passage of the Education Act, which granted the right to schooling to any male between the ages of 5 and 13.

American "**public schools**" are not to be confused with British public schools. The latter are private, whereas their American counterparts are indeed public—funded and directed by local authorities, open to all, and free.

Our public schools are run by local authorities in states, cities, and towns, which determine what is taught and who teaches it. There is some federal funding, but most of the costs of schools are raised by local governments through taxation. Schooling is free, including books and other teaching aids. And, except for some rare cases, students do not wear uniforms.

Originally, our schools were founded to teach the "**Three Rs**"—**reading, writing, and 'rithmetic** (mathematics). But today's schools teach much more. The modern curriculum can include science, computer skills, and even sex education, as well as teaching children to be good citizens and how to relate to others. There is also more emphasis today on creative thinking than rote memory and factual knowledge.

American schools have three stages. Elementary schools are grades 1 through 5 or 6; middle schools, grades 5 or 6 through 8; and high school, or secondary education, grades 9 to 12. Most local school districts also have a kindergarten, or preschool, free and open to all.

Public schools have traditionally been the responsibility of the states and local governments, but in an effort to improve public school education, particularly among disadvantaged children, the No Child Left Behind Act of 2001 greatly expanded the role of the federal government. Among its many provisions, the controversial law holds states and schools accountable for student progress, imposes annual tests in reading and mathematics for students in grades 3 to 8, requires states to bring all students up to the "proficient" level by the 2013–14 school year, mandates annual report cards showing student achievement, and stipulates that teachers be "highly qualified" in each subject they teach.

Our **private schools** are more like the British public schools. They are privately owned, charge for tuition and other costs, and their costs often approach those of private universities. Many of them are excellent, with high academic standards. Some also have religious affiliations and stress religiously-oriented teachings.

Charter schools, a recent and controversial development, are a hybrid. Publicly funded, they are non-sectarian elementary or secondary schools that are free from some of the rules and regulations that apply to public schools. In exchange, they are required to produce for the local or state government that issues the charter certain results for their students, as set forth in their charter.

A distinctive feature of American schools are the Parent-Teacher Associations (PTAs), which bring parents and teachers together on a regular basis to improve education in their local schools. PTAs also serve as starting points for political careers. Sen. Patty Murray began hers as a member of her local PTA and went on to serve as president of her local school board and member of the Washington State Senate before being elected to the U.S. Senate in 1992, and reelected in 1998 and 2004 despite being called by her opponents "a soccer mom in tennis shoes."

Another feature of American schools are provisions for ensuring education services throughout the nation to children with disabilities. The Individuals with Disabilities Education Act (IDEA) of 2004, the most recent of such laws, governs how states and public agencies provide early intervention, **special education** and related services. The history of the IDEA goes back to 1975, when Congress enacted the first federal law mandating education of children with disabilities, known as the Education for All Handicapped Children Act.

Higher education, like many other aspects of American life, is diverse. Some universities are colleges, and some colleges are universities, so don't go by the name alone; see what faculties they have, degrees they award, and by whom they are recognized or accredited. In general, colleges award only a Bachelor degree whereas universities award Bachelor, Masters, and Doctorates. Some are public, i.e. state universities or colleges, and others are private. Some are religious and others secular.

Community colleges, a recent innovation in higher education, offer a two-year curriculum leading to either the associate degree or transfer to a four-year college. The transfer program parallels the first two years of a four-year college. The degree program prepares students for direct entrance to an occupation. Because of their low tuition, local setting, and relatively easy entrance requirements, community colleges have been a major force in the post-World War II expansion of educational opportunities in the United States.

An emphasis on the liberal arts in undergraduate years, rather than technical skills, is what distinguishes American colleges from higher education in many other countries. Our undergraduates, for the most part, study literature, philosophy, history, and the other social sciences, in preparation for career choices in law, business, medicine, and the sciences, all of which are pursued in graduate schools.

In higher education, foreign students find our undergraduate colleges less rigorous than expected and the students less mature. American universities, however, which combine teaching with research, are greatly admired worldwide. But what often puzzles visitors from abroad is that our colleges and universities are not free, and students must pay a variety of fees. Full tuition, and room and board, at an elite private university can cost as much as $45,000 a year. Frequently overlooked, however, is that a wide range of scholarships are available, as well as loans that can be repaid after the student has graduated and become gainfully employed. Scholarships do not have to be repaid, but loans do, and with interest. At private four-year colleges, nearly three-quarters of students graduate with some debt to be repaid. At public universities, the figure is closer to 60 percent.

Gaining admission to a highly regarded college or university can be a trying experience for a high (secondary) school graduate. Admissions are based on a variety of factors, including among others, the grades and recommendations of high school teachers, results of the SAT (Scholastic Aptitude Test) similar to the "leaving exam" of European and other countries, extra curricular activities, athletic prowess, and family connections with the college. Since prestigious institutions admit only a small percentage of their applicants, competition is keen, and applicants will usually apply to several institutions to ensure acceptance by one of them.

For most American students, higher education, or college as it is commonly called, is a defining experience—their first time away from home and parental supervision. It's a time to meet new people from different backgrounds and origins, to make new friends who will last a lifetime, to study with professors who have ideas different from those of their students, and to join groups with a variety of new interests. It is also a time for experimentation, hence the presence of marijuana, alcohol, radical groups, and sex on college **campuses**.

THE RIGHTEOUS AMERICAN

... the religious atmosphere of the country was the first thing that struck me on arrival in the United States.
—Alexis de Tocqueville, *Democracy in America*

Difference of opinion is helpful in religion.
—Thomas Jefferson, 3rd U.S. President

Visitors to America express astonishment at the number of churches they see here and the large role they play in American life and politics. As a foreign visitor once asked me, "Why do you have so many different churches here in the United States?"

Such puzzlement is understandable for people who come from a country where one religion is recognized as dominant. In Russia, it's the Russian Orthodox Church; in neighboring Poland, Roman Catholic; and in Scandinavia, Lutheran. Germany is divided between Lutheran and Roman Catholic, and in Britain, it's the Church of England, known worldwide as the Anglican Communion, but in the United States as the Episcopal Church.

But perhaps nowhere else as in America are there so many different churches and religions. At some street intersections in our cities, you will see one church on each corner. In the Washington, D.C. suburbs, there is an avenue where, along one stretch of the road, there are more than thirty houses of worship. Among them are twenty-one different Protestant churches, three Catholic, one Ukrainian, two Seventh-Day Adventist, two Jehovah's Witnesses, one synagogue, a mosque, a Buddhist temple, a Hindu temple, as well as several others which do not have their own houses of worship but share houses with other religious groups. And all of these are located along only ten miles (sixteen kilometers) of the road.

The multiplicity of religions and churches in America is easily explained. People who came to America from many parts of the world brought their religions with them. Moreover, America has complete separation of church and state. There is no state church, and people are free to dissent from established religions and to break away and form their own. As the First Amendment to the Constitution provides:

> Congress shall make no law respecting an establishment
> of religion, or prohibiting the free exercise thereof; or
> abridging the freedom of speech, or of the press; or the
> right of the people peaceably to assemble, and to peti-
> tion the Government for a redress of grievances.

That is also the basis of the U.S. policy of strict separation of church and state.

About 80 percent of Americans identify themselves as Christian, and yet, as author Jon Meacham, puts it, "… the Founders constructed the first system of government in the world that allowed religion to flourish but not dominate …The good news about America—the gospel, if you will—is that many believe in God but no one must."[14] Religion in America is a matter of choice. Meacham quotes James Madison, one of our "**Founding Fathers**," saying that law was meant to comprehend, with the mantle of its protection, "the Jew and the Gentile, the Christian and the Mahometan, the Hindoo and infidel of every denomination."[15] The spelling has changed, but

---

14. *New York Times Book Review*, 25 December 2005.
15. John Meacham, *American Gospel: God, the Founding Fathers, and the Making of a Nation* (New York: Random House, 2006).

after more than 200 years the idea has not, and the various religious groups continue to play an extraordinarily strong role in what Americans call "**Civil Society**." And despite the separation of church and state, each session of the Senate and House of Representatives opens with a prayer offered by the chaplain of the Senate and House. A more divisive issue has been the offering of prayers at some high school football games and graduations, a recent trend that strict separationists, in keeping with another long-standing American tradition, have contested in the courts. Also contested in the courts and not yet fully resolved, is the inclusion of two words, "under God," in the Pledge of Allegiance to the Flag, a pledge usually recited at the daily opening of schools and at other public events. The pledge now reads "*I pledge allegiance to the Flag of the United States of America, and to the Republic for which it stands, one Nation under God, indivisible, with liberty and justice for all.*" However, in a typically American compromise, pledgers to the flag may omit the words "under God."

For those who are curious about numbers, the Roman Catholic Church, with more than 69 million members, is the largest religion in the United States. Second is the Southern Baptist, with 16.3 million members. Third is the United Methodist Church with just over 8 million.[16] Christians, with Protestants predominating, are the largest group, numbering some 80 percent, followed by those who do not profess a religion at 15 percent. Among the remaining 5 percent are Buddhists, Jews, and Muslims, among others. Yet, many of those who profess to adhere to a recognized church or religion are not true believers, and are more correctly called "New Age" adherents, a trend in contemporary America that is spiritual as well as religious, and explores religious traditions of both East and West.

Much as in distant millennia when many aspects of the pagan past became a part of our recognized religions, some elements of "New Age" religions have drawn inspiration from such

---

16. *Yearbook of American and Canadian Churches*, 2007. Published by the National Council of Churches.

beliefs as diverse as Spiritualism, Buddhism, Hinduism, Taoism, Shamanism, Wicca, and Neo-Paganism, as well as astrology, numerology, Kabbala, yoga, meditation, alternative medicine, and Sufism. As the opening song of the 1967 musical "Hair" told us, we have truly entered the "Age of Aquarius."[17]

---

17. An astrological era, Aquarius, being the 11th sign of the zodiac, is believed to have brought increased harmony and spirituality to the world.

WOMEN'S RIGHTS

The problem lay buried, unspoken, for many years in the minds of American women. It was a strange stirring, a sense of dissatisfaction, a yearning that women suffered in the middle of the twentieth century in the United States. Each suburban wife struggled with it alone. As she made the beds, shopped for groceries, matched slipcover material, ate peanut butter sandwiches with her children, chauffeured Cub Scouts and Brownies, lay beside her husband at night—she was afraid to ask even of herself the silent question—"Is this all?"
—Betty Friedan, *The Feminine Mystique*

Betty Friedan's book, *The Feminine Mystique*, published in 1963, started a movement that transformed the status of women in America.[18] **"Women's liberation,"** as it came to be called, opened the way to equal career opportunities in many fields previously denied to women—academia, business, the clergy, government, and the military, among others. It also gave birth to the campaign for legalized abortion in America.

During the same years, the sexual revolution in Europe reached America and brought with it changes in family, marriage, and child-bearing practices, as well as attitudes toward

---

18. Betty Friedan, *The Feminine Mystique* (New York: Dell, 1963).

women in general. Pregnancy before marriage became more common. Abortion, despite continued opposition, was found to be legal by the Supreme Court in the landmark 1973 case, *Roe v Wade*, and is now the law of the land.

These days, however, although not the norm, two groups of single women are now having children out of wedlock—those who fail to practice "**safe sex**" but for religious or other reasons decide not to have an abortion, and those who choose to have children by themselves, wishing to raise the child as a single parent rather than never have children at all. Casual sex is more common, but the threat of AIDS is making most informed people cautious about having unprotected sex.

Women's rights, often mislabeled as "feminism," have become a hot political and economic issue, as various women's organizations fight for equal rights for women and an end to gender discrimination. In recent years, women have become better educated, more competitive in the job market, and better paid. As a result, they today hold high positions in politics and the business world.

The effort for equal rights has even reached the restroom. In what has become jokingly known as "**potty parity**," construction standards are being changed to increase the number of women's toilets in order to shorten the long lines for women waiting patiently at theaters, concerts, sports events, and highway rest stops.

Prudery, nevertheless, persists, and bare breasts are still taboo, as is frontal nudity, even at beaches. Breast feeding in public has become accepted in some localities, if mothers are modest and cover up. But small children do not urinate in the streets, as they are allowed to do in many countries, and usually wear diapers instead.

As readers of these pages may have noticed, writers, recognizing that women may be half of their readers, are now using "he or she" and "his or hers," rather than just "he" and "his." Old habits die hard, but visitors should also be aware that "Ms." can indicate a single or a married woman, while "Miss" still indicates an unmarried, and "Mrs." a married woman.

SEX AND THE SINGLE VISITOR

You mustn't force sex to do the work of love or love to do the work of sex.

— Mary McCarthy, American writer

If you, the visitor, are thinking of getting married in America, you should look at the statistics before you leap. The "**stats**," as they are often called, favor women.

Citing the U.S. Census Bureau, the *New York Times* reports that "... among single non-Hispanic whites in their 20s, there are 120 men for every 100 women. The comparable figures are 153 Hispanic men, 132 Asian men, and 92 African American men for every 100 single women in their 20s of the same race or ethnicity.[19] And overall "... there are 120 men in their 20s who have never been married, widowed or divorced, for every 100 women in the same category."[20] Nonetheless, concludes the *Times*, the vast majority of Americans do get married, although, again according to the U.S. Census, married households are not a majority. And, adds the *Times*, "More people are living together without marrying; more are marrying people of another race. And more women are choosing motherhood without marrying."

---

19. *New York Times*, 12 February 2006.
20. Ibid.

So, if you are looking for a "**partner**" or "**significant other**" here, as companions are now called, where do you meet people of the opposite, or same, sex? The answer, for men, is almost everywhere, because women now can be found in almost every line of work, and many of them are looking for men. Consider also organizations that sponsor what are called "**leisure activities**," such as health clubs and educational institutions that conduct classes in everything from cooking to gardening.

One sure place to look is the "**Personals**" or "**In Search Of**" advertisements in newspapers and magazines, or on certain websites. Many places of worship welcome singles, and quite a few have singles clubs. For those who are seeking a little adventure, there are dance clubs which have a bar, dance floor, **DJ**, and sometimes live music. You can even find a partner on the Internet, which has several sites for singles. Good luck! But because there are married men who prey on unsuspecting single women, there are also websites that will do a background check on a potential suitor and verify his marital status, age, address, and criminal record.

Marrying an American, however, may not be so easy. Americans are marrying later in life, and living single has become more common. In Boston, for example, 53.6 percent of the men and 45 percent of the women have never married. The figures for Newark, New Jersey, and Washington, D.C. are similar. In all such cities, single people are not opposed to marriage; they are just waiting for the right person to come along, and they are prepared to wait.[21]

But remember the advice of the Frenchman who was looking for the perfect woman. When he finally found her, much to his disappointment, she was looking for the perfect man.

The feminist movement has opened many career opportunities for women, and as a result, American women have become more self-sufficient, able to support themselves and even buy a home. The high divorce rate, approaching 50 percent,

---

21. *Boston Globe*, 4 June 2006.

has also made women and men more cautious about marriage. If current divorce rates continue, half of all young adults will get divorced over the course of their lifetimes.

Homosexuality has become more and more accepted and protected by legislation as gays and lesbians have become a political force in both the Democratic and Republican Parties. Some American states have passed laws recognizing marriages or "**civil unions**" between same-sex couples but other states have outlawed them. The traditional family, however, continues to flourish, and the vast majority of Americans do get married. With the acceptance of "**no-fault divorce**" in many states, however, the likelihood of a marriage leading to divorce is coming closer to 50 percent.[22]

As in Europe and some other parts of the world, the treatment of sex on television and film has become more graphic. Part of this is related to business—sex sells—witness all the advertisements with "**sex appeal**" in newspapers and on TV. But it is also due to more liberal attitudes by the public toward sex, nudity, and language that was once considered to be obscene or vulgar.

Sex does sell, but sexually transmitted diseases (STDs) remain a major public health challenge in the United States and many other countries. While substantial progress has been made in preventing, diagnosing, and treating certain STDs in recent years, the U.S. government Centers for Disease Control (CDC) estimates that approximately 19 million new infections occur each year in the United States, almost half of them among young people ages 15 to 24.

---

22. A no-fault divorce is one in which neither spouse blames the other for the marriage breakdown. Both spouses agree that irreconcilable differences have arisen, and that neither time nor counseling will save the marriage.

LAWS AND LAWYERS

We are a nation of laws, not men.
— popular quote

When Richard Nixon was elected president in 1968, a Russian professor of law in Moscow asked me why there were so many lawyers in the new president's cabinet. Lawyers were not prominent in the Soviet Union, and their role in American politics surprised him.

I gave him the standard textbook answer—we are "a nation of laws, not men." A better answer might have been a quote from Abraham Lincoln, the 16th U.S. President: "Let reverence for the laws … become the political religion of the nation."

Reverence for the law is a U. S. carryover from England, the mother country, where the Magna Carta (literally, Great Charter), issued originally in 1215, was the most significant early influence on the historical process that led to the rule of constitutional law today. The Magna Carta required the king to renounce certain rights, respect certain legal procedures and recognize that the will of the king could be bound by the law. It influenced common law such as the United States Constitution and **Bill of Rights** and is considered one of the most important legal documents in the history of democracy.

The English colonists in America brought with them the English system of courts, and even today the English heritage remains in America. Many of the old English terms are still with us, such as sheriff, bailiff, writ, *habeas corpus*, jury, and hearing.

Lawyers in America are respected, even held in awe, regarded as learned, and are second only to medical doctors in the unofficial **"pecking order"** of American professions. The legal profession also opens the door to upward mobility. Many young people from immigrant families have gone to law school, taken up politics, and entered the middle and upper classes of America. Lawyers are found everywhere, in business, government, education, and science. America is truly a nation of laws and lawyers.

Living with governmental regulations and limits is something to which Americans have become accustomed. There are laws limiting the size and shape of your house or apartment, the way you drive your car, the hours that you can eat or drink in restaurants, and the type of products you can buy in stores.

For business, laws have become enormously complex. In every area of legislation, the difficulty in understanding what is required has led to the development of legal specialists who can interpret legal requirements. The federal tax code, for example, is thousands of pages long; and each of the 50 states has its own tax laws that apply to business activities in its state. The difficulty of understanding all those requirements has resulted in an army of tax lawyers who do nothing but advise businesses on how to comply with, and obtain the most advantage from, the tax laws.

That complexity is found in many different areas. There are food and drug laws; environmental, health and safety laws; labor laws, corporate laws, property laws, criminal laws, and health laws. In most cases, there are very serious penalties—the risk of jail or very high fines—for those who disobey the laws. The result has been a high demand for lawyers who can safely guide businesses and individuals through the maze of complex requirements.

In 2005 there were more than one million lawyers in the United States, which comes to 341 lawyers for every 100,000

Americans. In our Congress, half of the senators and about one-third of the representatives are lawyers. They help write the laws that shape our government and by which we live.

But ordinary citizens also need lawyers, for advice on observing laws and regulations, drawing up contracts, purchasing a home or other property, writing a will, and for defense in lawsuits. We don't need a lawyer to get married but we do need one to get divorced, especially where property and support are involved.

"So sue me" is a phrase often used when people have a disagreement with another person. Our country is very **litigious** because both parties to a dispute know that they can go to a court at one of the three levels of American courts—local, state, and federal—and get an honest and impartial judgment.

Lawyers are often criticized and made the butt of jokes, until you need one. You will have to pay for the advice—most lawyers charge by the hour—but the advice you get will usually be worth the cost, and because we live according to laws, it will save you a lot of trouble and money.

But remember, when you talk to a lawyer, his clock is ticking.

TONS OF GUNS

A well-regulated Militia, being necessary to the security of a free State, the right of the people to keep and bear arms, shall not be infringed.
—Second Amendment to the U.S. Constitution

Many foreign visitors find America's love affair with guns puzzling. Forty percent of U.S. households have a firearm, and if all the guns in the country were spread around, there would be one for every 916 men, women, and children out of 1,000.[23] Criminals on our streets have guns, as do law-abiding people in their homes, and as a result we have the highest rate of handgun deaths—about 40,000 a year, by murder, suicide, and accidents—among the world's thirty-six richest nations. Why do so many Americans want guns?

Many want guns to protect themselves from criminals. Others want them for hunting or sport shooting. And some want them because they have a fascination with firearms.

In our Constitution, dating from the year 1791, there is a Second Amendment provision: "… the right of the people to keep and bear arms shall not be infringed." However, there is disagreement over what that actually means.

---

23. *Washington Post*, 26 April 2006.

One interpretation argues that the right to bear arms is a collective one, existing only for the purpose of maintaining an effective militia, called in America "The **National Guard**." The Supreme Court's long-standing interpretation of the Second Amendment was that the individual's right to bear arms applied only to the preservation or efficiency of a well-regulated militia, and except for lawful police and military purposes, the possession of weapons by individuals was not constitutionally protected. But in June 2008, the Supreme Court, in a 5-to-4 decision, struck down a law of the District of Columbia, the nation's capital, which banned handguns, and the Court, for the first time in the nation's history, said that the Second Amendment guarantees an individual's right to own a gun for self defense. The Court, however, left open the question of how such ownership can be regulated.

Public opinion polls show that a majority of Americans favor some kind of handgun regulation by government. But other Americans fiercely defend their right to "keep and bear" arms, and that right is defended by the National Rifle Association (NRA), a non-governmental organization (NGO) that represents gun owners, gun retailers, and the gun manufacturing industry. One result is that some states and cities have adopted laws on who can own and carry a handgun, while other states and cities have not.

For visitors, this means that your right to bear arms may depend on which state or municipality you visit. So, if you must carry a gun, check to see what the local law says, and observe the regulations. In any event, carrying a gun on an airplane is fully forbidden.

Racism

I swear to the Lord
I still can't see
Why Democracy means
Everybody but me.

—Langston Hughes, "The Black Man Speaks"

Racism is as old as mankind. It has been practiced in many places around the world where people of one culture or color have come in contact with another in their migrations due to wars, famines, or weather changes. Only recently has the term "race" been replaced by "ethnicity," but the results have been the same. Ethnic minorities, **aka** "the others," have been singled out for discrimination in many countries, and the United States has been no exception.

Despite the lofty and well-intentioned words of the Declaration of Independence, the U.S. Constitution, and the Bill of Rights, and victories by the liberal-minded in the U.S. Courts and the Congress, there nevertheless have been recurring acts of discrimination, official and non-official, in American history. Among them have been the treatment of Native Americans, the enslavement of blacks, the rampages of the Ku Klux Klan, anti-Asian immigration measures, anti-Catholic prejudice, anti-Semitism, internment of Japanese-Americans during World War II, and, more recently, anti-Hispanic sentiment across the United States.

However, the charges of racism in the United States that have received the most attention have been those raised by the black community. As a friend of mine from Africa, who is a tenured professor at an American college and has a doctorate from a major university, has put it, he did not know that he was black until he arrived in the United States, and here he has been reminded of it every day. He describes it as a challenge to his dignity.

The U.S. civil rights legislation of the 1950s and 1960s overturned a number of legal decisions and practices which, in effect, had condoned racial segregation and discrimination against blacks, especially in the southern states.[24]

The landmark *Brown v Board of Education* decision of the U.S. Supreme Court in 1954 ended the "separate but equal" legal doctrine which had permitted separate schools for American blacks. Subsequent legislation banned discrimination in employment practices, public accommodations (service in restaurants, hotels, etc.), sale or rental of housing, and restored voting rights. Nevertheless, disparities still exist between blacks and whites, and they are largely economic and educational.

According to U.S. Census Bureau statistics of 2005, three-fourths of white households owned their own homes while only 46 percent of blacks did. Thirty percent of white adults had at least a bachelor's degree and only 17 percent of black adults did. And while the median income for white households was $50,622, it was $30,939 for blacks.[25] The differences, however, were not only in economics and education but included crime. Nearly half of the nation's murder victims in 2005 were black, and a black man between the ages of 18 and 24 is more than eight times as likely as a white man of the same age group to be murdered.[26] As Dr. Alvin Poussaint, a Professor of Psychiatry at Harvard Medical School, has pointed out:

---

24. African Americans, or "blacks" or "people of color," as they currently prefer to be called, were formerly called Negroes or "colored." Under no circumstances should "nigger," commonly called the "n word," be used.
25. *Washington Post*, 14 November 2006.
26. *Washington Post*, editorial, 28 November 2007.

In Baltimore, 76 percent of black males don't graduate from high school. Of the two million people in jail [in the United States], about 45 percent are African-American, most have been males. Of the homicides in the country, about 45 percent are African-American males, mostly killing other black people and black males.[27]

Bill Cosby, a leading black comedian, movie actor, and TV star, is also angry, and he blames the African-American community for its juvenile delinquency, poor parenting, and the coarse language of its youth. "You can do better," he exhorts his audiences. "Don't let yourself be victims, and especially don't let the poorest in the community let themselves be victims."

"This is about little children … and people not giving them better choices," Cosby told Paula Zahn in an interview with CNN. "Talking. Talking. Parenting. Correctly parenting. That's what it's about. And you can't blame other things. You got to— you got to straighten up your house. Straighten up your apartment. Straighten up your child."[28]

Cosby's remarks, which stirred up much controversy in the black community, were defended by Juan Williams, a leading black journalist:

> Cosby's point is that lost, poor black people have suffered most from not having strong leaders. His charge is that these leaders — cultural and political — misinform, mismanage, and miseducate by refusing to articulate established truths about what it takes to get ahead: strong families, education, and hard work …. Who will tell you that if you want to get a job you have to stay in school and spend more money on education than on disposable consumer goods? Where are the black leaders who are willing to stand tall and say that any black man who wants to be a success has to speak proper English?[29]

27. Lehrer News Hour, 15 July 2004.
28. Bill Cosby, Interview with Paula Zahn, CNN.com, 12 November 2004.
29. Juan Williams, "Morning Edition," National Public Radio, 7 August 2006.

Yes, there is still racism in the United States, but for those who are willing to apply themselves, it should not be an insurmountable obstacle to achieving success.

As French author Bernard-Henri Lévy has observed:

> There is a gentleness, a lightness, an element of freedom and, in a word, of civilization, that makes this country one of the few countries in the world where, despite everything, you can still breathe freely.[30]

---

30. Bernard-Henri Lévy, *American Vertigo.*

MESSIANIC MISSION

The world must be made safe for democracy.
—Woodrow Wilson, 28th U.S. President, 2 April 1917

So it is the policy of the United States to seek and support the growth of democratic movements and institutions in every nation and culture, with the ultimate goal of ending tyranny in our world.
—George W. Bush, 43rd U.S. President, 20 January 2005

Eighty-four years separate the statements of two U.S. presidents on America's mission in the world but the idea is the same—America has an obligation to bring enlightenment and democracy to the rest of the world. Wilson, the son of a Presbyterian minister, came to office with a confidence that God was guiding him. Bush, a Methodist and **"born again" Christian**, similarly stated that he and the nation were on a divinely guided mission. As Bush put it, "We have a calling from beyond the stars to stand for freedom."[31]

The United States is not alone in claiming such an ambitious mission. France has long laid claim to its *mission civilisatrice*, designed to spread French culture and influence abroad. England left a legacy of law, government, free trade,

---

31. www.whitehouse.gov, 19 January 2005.

and the English language in many of its former colonies. Russia, during its tsarist era, spoke of its civilizing mission across Eurasia, and the Russian authorities continue to speak of it today.

Divine missions and strong national pride have been guiding principles in many countries, and America is no exception. But the unique status of the United States as the only remaining superpower lends support to the idea among American policymakers and the public that one historian calls "a restorative myth of national origins": one that encourages us in the conviction that we are a nation uniquely blessed by God and that we have reached a level of righteousness unattained by any other country.[32] America's policies, values, and virtues, this line of thought tells us, have been vindicated by history. As a consequence, Americans tend to be very sensitive to any implied criticism of their country.

Yet despite that worldwide messianic mission, most Americans are woefully uninformed about the world beyond our borders. Less than 25 percent of Americans currently possess passports. Most newspapers, with the exception of those in large cities, carry little foreign news, and television and radio, with the exception of the Public Broadcasting System and National Public Radio, do no better.

The study of foreign languages in public schools and universities has declined. As a popular saying puts it:

> If you can speak three languages you're trilingual. If you can speak two languages you're bilingual. If you can speak only one language you're an American.

Nevertheless, more than 300 languages are spoken in America, of which 176 are indigenous. And while 82 percent of Americans are native speakers of English, 47 million of them speak another language at home, mostly Spanish. Large parts of America once spoke other languages—French in New Eng-

32. Nathanial Philbrick, quoted by Jonathan Yardley in *Washington Post Book World*, 7 May 2006.

land and Louisiana, German in Pennsylvania, Scandinavian languages in our upper Midwest, and Spanish throughout our Southwest. And today we have many new immigrants speaking Russian, Polish, Cantonese and Mandarin, Vietnamese, and Korean, as well as Dari, Pashto, Hindi, Bengali, Wolof, and Swahili. Our society is becoming polyglot.

Some Americans feel threatened by Spanish, and this has given rise to a movement to make English the national language, meaning that all government business would have to be conducted in English. Such movements have come and gone before in America's history following waves of arriving immigrants speaking other languages, and this one will likely be no exception, as we have come to realize that we do indeed have a language problem.

Belatedly, America has come to recognize that the significant gaps in foreign language skills among too many of us are indeed a handicap. As a remedy, President George W. Bush called for a national program to encourage the study of Arabic, Chinese, Russian, Hindi, Farsi, and other languages that are rarely studied here. As the *New York Times* reported, a study in 2005 that resulted from a gathering of leaders in government, industry, and academia concluded that large gaps in language skills have threatened the country's safety and competitiveness. "They have restrained social mobility, lessened our commercial competitiveness, limited the effectiveness of public diplomacy, and restricted justice and government services to sectors of our society," the report said. "And they have threatened national security."[33]

More and more young Americans, however, are going abroad to study. Though only 1 percent of students are currently studying abroad at some time during their college years, the number has been increasing from year to year. In 2007 there were 223,534 American students studying abroad, up from about 75,000 thirteen years earlier.[34]

To give a further impetus to that trend, the U.S. Senate

33. *New York Times*, 6 January 2006.
34. Open Doors 2007, Institute of International Education, New York, 2007.

unanimously passed a bipartisan resolution designating 2006 as the "Year of Study Abroad."[35]

A sense of superiority, however, still prevails. Many Americans see the United States as the model for the rest of the world and assume that everyone wants to come here to live. There is a sense of "America—love it or leave it," and "My country—right or wrong;" and if something is not American, it must be of lesser quality or importance.

Yet despite our history of isolation from the rest of the world, there is also a history of America coming to the aid of other countries in distress. Americans look back with pride at their generous assistance to other countries in times of need. When famine hit Russia in 1921-22, after six and one-half years of World War I, revolution, and civil war, the United States led an international effort that avoided mass starvation for more than ten million people, with most of the food funded by the U.S. Congress. For the Marshall Plan, which was instrumental in the recovery of Europe after World War II, America spent more than 10 percent of its federal budget. America has also been quick to respond to other disasters around the world. Most recently, after the Asian tsunami of 2004, the United States responded with $907.3 million in long-term support for victims in many of the affected Asian countries.

---

35. *Foreign Service Journal* (June 2006), 65.

DISSIDENCE OR INTOLERANCE?

Give me your tired, your poor,
Your huddled masses yearning to breathe free,
The wretched refuse of your teeming shore.
Send these, the homeless, tempest-tost to me,
I lift my lamp beside the golden door!

—Emma Lazarus, 1883

More than 124 years after they were written, the lines of Emma Lazarus's poem, "The New Colossus," engraved on a plaque in New York Harbor's Statue of Liberty, continue to inspire newcomers to the United States. And the newcomers continue to come.

The U.S. Census Bureau estimates that with a baby being born every 8 seconds, a death every 12 seconds, and the nation gaining an immigrant every 31 seconds on average, the U.S. population is growing by one person every 14 seconds (and had passed 300 million by the end of 2006).[36] Based on current trends the Census Bureau projects a U.S. population of 363,584,435 in the year 2030, a 23 percent increase over the 294 million estimate on January 1, 2006.[37] And that is hap-

---

36. *New York Times*, 13 January, 2006.
37. *Washington Post*, 1 January, 2006.

pening while the populations of most European countries are declining.

With the population growing, our tradition of independent thought, and with people coming to our shores from so many different places, there is bound to be an increase in dissidents, people who disagree with the conventional wisdom. That might include political refugees from many countries around the world, or those who hold unpopular views in their home countries, or people who are seeking religious freedom, as were the Pilgrims from England who settled in Plymouth, Massachusetts in 1620. And then there are those Americans whose views are not politically correct. We are indeed a nation of dissidents, some of whom hold views or support movements that are decidedly intolerant.

The Ku Klux Klan was a fraternal organization that arose in the American South after the Civil War. Advocating white supremacy, it resorted to violence and the burning of crosses to intimidate African Americans. Its membership has risen and fallen over the years up to the present as it has advocated, at various times, racism, anti-Semitism, anti-Catholicism, and homophobia.

The Know Nothing movement was a nativist political movement of the 1850s formed in reaction to fears that major cities were being overwhelmed by Irish Catholic immigrants who were regarded as hostile to American values and controlled by the Pope in Rome. A short-lived movement mainly active 1854 to 1856, it demanded reform measures but few were passed. Its membership, mainly middle class and Protestant, was soon absorbed by other political parties.

In the late 19th century, the immigration of Chinese workers to the United States was opposed by a movement associated with the racist phrase, the so-called "**yellow peril**," and the fear that the mass immigration of Asians would threaten white wages, standards of living, and Western civilization itself. The term "yellow peril" was common in the newspapers owned by William Randolph Hearst.

Anti-Semitism reared its ugly head in the 1930s with the

German-American Bund, a Nazi-like organization, and the rabble-rousing rhetoric of Father Charles Coughlin, a Catholic radio priest, until his controversial economic populist broadcasts and vitriolic attacks on President Franklin D. Roosevelt were silenced by his Church superiors.

Thousands of Japanese Americans were held in camps during World War II, although there is not a single documented case of sabotage or espionage committed by a Japanese American during that time, and despite the fact that many Japanese Americans served with distinction in our military during the war. It was not until 1988 that an official apology and financial redress were forthcoming from the U.S. government.

In our own time, as a spillover of the violence and terrorism emanating from the Middle East, we have seen a rise in anti-Muslim sentiment among some Americans.

Such examples of intolerance have surfaced in American history from time to time but, seen as violations of basic civil rights, they have not lasted very long nor been accepted by mainstream politics.

Illustrative is the case of the National Socialist Party of America, a very small neo-Nazi movement which in 1977 announced its intention to march in the mostly Jewish village of Skokie, Illinois, a suburb of Chicago. Village officials obtained a court order against the demonstration and took additional steps to ban the planned protest. The neo-Nazis called on the **American Civil Liberties Union** (ACLU), a leading civil rights organization, to defend them against the violation of their rights to free speech under the U.S. Constitution. To the surprise of many, the ACLU agreed that a violation had indeed occurred, and it took up the defense of the neo-Nazis. Three thousand ACLU members resigned in protest, but as a lawyer for the ACLU put it:

> We are in the business of supporting the first amendment. We do not support the ideas of this particular organization, nor have we ever, nor will we ever. But the issue is not the content of their views, the question is

what is the power of government to pick and choose among speakers in the marketplace of ideas?

The neo-Nazis, who got the restoration of their First Amendment rights to speak and assemble, called off their Skokie march, and only a handful of them showed up for the demonstration. Far outnumbered by opponents, they completed their march and left under police protection. Shortly thereafter their organization faded away.

GOVERNMENT

The character inherent in the American people has done all that has been accomplished; and it would have done somewhat more, if the government had not sometimes got in its way.

— Henry David Thoreau, American writer

Together with the American emphasis on privacy and the individual, there is also a deep distrust of concentrated authority and a strong belief that government should interfere as little as possible in the lives of the people. As a Dutch visitor commented, despite their large bureaucracy, Americans enjoy much more personal freedom than Europeans. That view is reflected in a popular saying: "The government that governs least, governs best."

Consequently, there is a continuing debate in American political life about the role of government. How much should it interfere in the lives of individuals, or in business or the economic and social affairs of the country, in order to protect society as a whole and, in particular, the poor, the sick, and the old? That debate separates Republicans from Democrats, and liberals from conservatives. It also separates those who favor a strong federal government in Washington, D.C. and those who support the rights of the fifty states.

Compared to many governments around the world, however, the influence of the American federal bureaucracy is much less prevalent. The United States does not have an internal passport or national identification document (ID). A driver's license, issued by a state or other photo ID will usually suffice for identification. And you don't have to register with the police when you move to another location or stay in a hotel.

The war on terrorism has resulted in increased surveillance, but if you do not engage in any illegal or suspicious activities in America, or do not make a telephone call to a terrorist, "**Big Brother**" should not be watching you.

In contrast to most other democracies, America does not have a proportional representation system of politics. It's winner takes all for the party that gets more than 50 percent of the vote in elections for the two branches of Congress—the **House of Representatives** and the **Senate**. Nevertheless, the minority party, even without a majority of votes in the Congress, can often delay or alter legislation proposed by the majority party which it opposes.

The thirteen English colonies that became the United States of America had lived under the total power of the English king, and it is understandable that our **Founding Fathers**, as they are known, would want to prevent a concentration of power in one government official or office.[38] The Constitution they adopted serves not only to establish the rules of governance, but also to protect the individual citizen from the power of the government.

Accordingly, the Constitution created three branches for the federal government—**legislative**, **executive**, and **judicial**—with separate responsibilities so that power would be restrained under what is called a system of "**checks and balances**." No single branch of government can become too powerful because it is balanced by the other two branches. However, the Congress is described in the first article of the Constitution, which

---

38. Here I have drawn from http://uscis.gov/graphics/citizenship/learning.htm, "Guide for New Immigrants: Learning About the United States," a website of the U.S. Citizenship and Immigration Service which prepares immigrants for the examination of American history and civics they must take to become citizens.

would indicate that the Founding Fathers intended to give priority to the Congress, rather than to an all-powerful president to replace the English king they had rejected. And to protect individual citizen from the power of the state, a Bill of Rights was adopted to the Constitution, guaranteeing basic rights of citizens.

For the legislative branch, citizens of the United States vote in free elections to choose people to represent them in the U.S. Congress. The Congress, consisting of the House of Representatives and the Senate, has the responsibility for making laws and deciding how the government spends the money it takes in from taxes. As is said, "The president proposes but the congress disposes."

For the House of Representatives, residents of each state vote to elect the 435 members of the House, as it is commonly called. "Representatives" represent the people, and the number of representatives from each state is determined by how many people live in that state. States are divided into districts, and people living in each district vote for someone to represent them in the House. Representatives serve for two years, and then their constituents have another opportunity to either send their Representatives back to Washington, D.C. for another two years, or to vote for different persons to represent them. Representatives can serve in Congress for an unlimited number of terms.

The Senate, the senior branch of the Congress, represents the fifty states. People in each state vote to choose two Senators to represent them in the Congress. Senators serve for six years, and then voters have another chance to vote for them again or for to choose a different person to represent their state. Senators can also serve for an unlimited number of terms, but one-third of the senators are elected every two years so there is less likelihood of a dramatic shift of power from one party to the other. Senators make laws, and they also have additional responsibilities.

The Senate can approve or disapprove treaties the President makes with other countries or organizations of countries. The

Senate also can say "yes" or "no," confirming or rejecting persons the President chooses for high-level jobs, such as **Supreme Court** justices, ambassadors, and officials to head the various federal departments, called ministries in most other countries. The Senate can also hold a trial for a government official who is charged with committing a crime against the United States.

Legislation must be approved by both the House and the Senate. But when the two chambers differ on the provisions of a law they have approved, they go into "Conference," as it is called, to reconcile the differences through the time-tested procedure of compromise. However, Congress can override a presidential veto with a two-thirds vote in the House and the Senate.

The President heads the Executive Branch and is responsible for upholding and enforcing the laws of the country. The President also may approve or disapprove (called a "veto") laws passed by the Congress. However, the Congress may override a presidential veto with a two-thirds vote in the Senate and the House. The President has many other responsibilities, such as setting national policies, proposing laws to Congress, and choosing high-level officials as well as members of the Supreme Court. The President also is the leader of the U.S. military and bears the title of Commander-in-Chief. People vote in elections for the President and Vice President every four years, but the President can serve in office for only two four-year terms. If the President becomes disabled or dies, the Vice President becomes President.

The Judicial Branch, the third branch of government, is the final arbiter of political issues. To quote de Tocqueville once more: "There is hardly a political question in the United States that does not sooner or later turn into a judicial one."[39] The Constitution created the Supreme Court, the highest court in the United States, which has nine Justices, as they are called. The President chooses the justices, who serve as long as they

---

39. Alexis de Tocqueville, *Democracy in America*.

are able. The Supreme Court can overrule both state and federal laws if it finds that they conflict with the Constitution, and it therefore has the final say on issues of law and the Constitution. There are also lower federal courts, such as U.S. District Courts and U.S. Circuit Courts. All federal courts are completely independent of other branches of the government.

This sounds complicated and unwieldy, and the system may be less efficient than a strong and centralized government. Indeed, many foreign observers have wondered how such a decentralized government, with its system of checks and balances and limitations on executive power, could become a superpower. Yet, that system of government, with its compromise-based deliberations, has persevered for more than 200 years, providing stability and an orderly transfer of power through national elections every two, four, and six years that represent the will of the people. "Democracy," as Winston Churchill said, "is the worst form of government, except for all those other forms that have been tried from time to time."

Americans are rather well-informed about their legal system. Court trials are frequent subjects of Hollywood movies and TV films, and most Americans may have to serve on a jury at some time in their adult life. As a consequence, most Americans have confidence in their legal system and are confident that justice will be done.

THE GOVERNMENT OF THE UNITED STATES

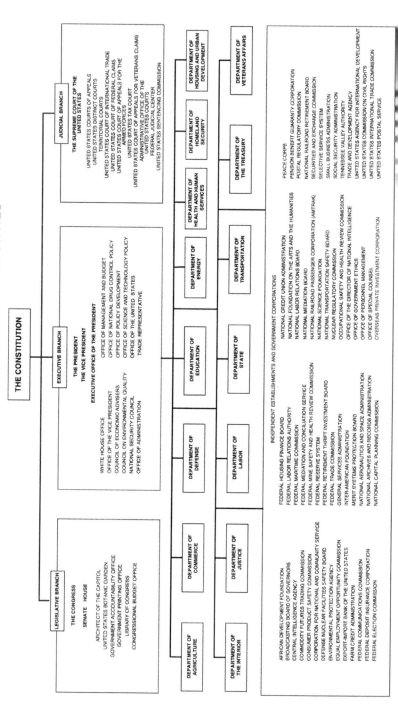

THE CONSTITUTION

LEGISLATIVE BRANCH

THE CONGRESS

SENATE   HOUSE

ARCHITECT OF THE CAPITOL
UNITED STATES BOTANIC GARDEN
GOVERNMENT ACCOUNTABILITY OFFICE
GOVERNMENT PRINTING OFFICE
LIBRARY OF CONGRESS
CONGRESSIONAL BUDGET OFFICE

EXECUTIVE BRANCH

THE PRESIDENT
THE VICE PRESIDENT

EXECUTIVE OFFICE OF THE PRESIDENT

WHITE HOUSE OFFICE
OFFICE OF THE VICE PRESIDENT
COUNCIL OF ECONOMIC ADVISERS
COUNCIL ON ENVIRONMENTAL QUALITY
NATIONAL SECURITY COUNCIL
OFFICE OF ADMINISTRATION

OFFICE OF MANAGEMENT AND BUDGET
OFFICE OF NATIONAL DRUG CONTROL POLICY
OFFICE OF POLICY DEVELOPMENT
OFFICE OF SCIENCE AND TECHNOLOGY POLICY
OFFICE OF THE UNITED STATES
TRADE REPRESENTATIVE

JUDICIAL BRANCH

THE SUPREME COURT OF THE
UNITED STATES

UNITED STATES COURTS OF APPEALS
UNITED STATES DISTRICT COURTS
TERRITORIAL COURTS
UNITED STATES COURT OF INTERNATIONAL TRADE
UNITED STATES COURT OF FEDERAL CLAIMS
UNITED STATES COURT OF APPEALS FOR THE
ARMED FORCES
UNITED STATES TAX COURT
UNITED STATES COURT OF APPEALS FOR VETERANS CLAIMS
ADMINISTRATIVE OFFICE OF THE
UNITED STATES COURTS
FEDERAL JUDICIAL CENTER
UNITED STATES SENTENCING COMMISSION

DEPARTMENT OF AGRICULTURE

DEPARTMENT OF COMMERCE

DEPARTMENT OF DEFENSE

DEPARTMENT OF EDUCATION

DEPARTMENT OF ENERGY

DEPARTMENT OF HEALTH AND HUMAN SERVICES

DEPARTMENT OF HOMELAND SECURITY

DEPARTMENT OF HOUSING AND URBAN DEVELOPMENT

DEPARTMENT OF THE INTERIOR

DEPARTMENT OF JUSTICE

DEPARTMENT OF LABOR

DEPARTMENT OF STATE

DEPARTMENT OF TRANSPORTATION

DEPARTMENT OF THE TREASURY

DEPARTMENT OF VETERANS AFFAIRS

INDEPENDENT ESTABLISHMENTS AND GOVERNMENT CORPORATIONS

AFRICAN DEVELOPMENT FOUNDATION
BROADCASTING BOARD OF GOVERNORS
CENTRAL INTELLIGENCE AGENCY
COMMODITY FUTURES TRADING COMMISSION
CONSUMER PRODUCT SAFETY COMMISSION
CORPORATION FOR NATIONAL AND COMMUNITY SERVICE
DEFENSE NUCLEAR FACILITIES SAFETY BOARD
ENVIRONMENTAL PROTECTION AGENCY
EQUAL EMPLOYMENT OPPORTUNITY COMMISSION
EXPORT-IMPORT BANK OF THE UNITED STATES
FARM CREDIT ADMINISTRATION
FEDERAL COMMUNICATIONS COMMISSION
FEDERAL DEPOSIT INSURANCE CORPORATION
FEDERAL ELECTION COMMISSION

FEDERAL HOUSING FINANCE BOARD
FEDERAL LABOR RELATIONS AUTHORITY
FEDERAL MARITIME COMMISSION
FEDERAL MEDIATION AND CONCILIATION SERVICE
FEDERAL MINE SAFETY AND HEALTH REVIEW COMMISSION
FEDERAL RESERVE SYSTEM
FEDERAL RETIREMENT THRIFT INVESTMENT BOARD
FEDERAL TRADE COMMISSION
GENERAL SERVICES ADMINISTRATION
INTER-AMERICAN FOUNDATION
MERIT SYSTEMS PROTECTION BOARD
NATIONAL AERONAUTICS AND SPACE ADMINISTRATION
NATIONAL ARCHIVES AND RECORDS ADMINISTRATION
NATIONAL CAPITAL PLANNING COMMISSION

NATIONAL CREDIT UNION ADMINISTRATION
NATIONAL FOUNDATION ON THE ARTS AND THE HUMANITIES
NATIONAL LABOR RELATIONS BOARD
NATIONAL MEDIATION BOARD
NATIONAL RAILROAD PASSENGER CORPORATION (AMTRAK)
NATIONAL SCIENCE FOUNDATION
NATIONAL TRANSPORTATION SAFETY BOARD
NUCLEAR REGULATORY COMMISSION
OCCUPATIONAL SAFETY AND HEALTH REVIEW COMMISSION
OFFICE OF THE DIRECTOR OF NATIONAL INTELLIGENCE
OFFICE OF GOVERNMENT ETHICS
OFFICE OF PERSONNEL MANAGEMENT
OFFICE OF SPECIAL COUNSEL
OVERSEAS PRIVATE INVESTMENT CORPORATION

PEACE CORPS
PENSION BENEFIT GUARANTY CORPORATION
POSTAL REGULATORY COMMISSION
RAILROAD RETIREMENT BOARD
SECURITIES AND EXCHANGE COMMISSION
SELECTIVE SERVICE SYSTEM
SMALL BUSINESS ADMINISTRATION
SOCIAL SECURITY ADMINISTRATION
TENNESSEE VALLEY AUTHORITY
TRADE AND DEVELOPMENT AGENCY
UNITED STATES AGENCY FOR INTERNATIONAL DEVELOPMENT
UNITED STATES COMMISSION ON CIVIL RIGHTS
UNITED STATES INTERNATIONAL TRADE COMMISSION
UNITED STATES POSTAL SERVICE

DEMOCRATS AND REPUBLICANS

I am not a member of any organized political party. I am a Democrat.
—Will Rogers, American humorist

During my many years abroad as a Foreign Service Officer, I was often asked to explain the difference between the Republican and Democratic Parties. Europeans, who have a wide range of parties from far left to far right, do not see much, if any, ideological differences between the two major American political parties. Both support representative government and the free enterprise system. They may differ, however, on many fundamental issues that affect every American—taxation, social issues, business and the economy, and international affairs. But as one Republican has put it, "… most Americans are now presented with a choice between two parties that are both addicted to power—the Democrats to governmental power and the Republicans to corporate and governmental power."[40]

Each party is actually a coalition of groups with a wide range of views, from liberal to conservative, reflecting the interests of their constituents and their political, economic, geographic, ethnic, religious, and environmental concerns. Prior to national elections, each party writes a "platform," as it is

---

40. Craig Shirley, "How the GOP Lost Its Way," *Washington Post*, 22 April 2006.

called, to state its positions on current issues. But those positions are not always closely observed in the legislative process when Representatives and Senators, as well as the Executive Branch, must make compromises to approve legislation which affects the major interests of their constituents.

In that legislative process, as well as in elections, both parties court the uncommitted voters, the so-called "**swing vote**," who are not members of either party but whose votes depend on the issues that concern them.

In recent years many Americans have become critical of the constant bickering between the two parties and have called for an end to partisan politics. But debate and arguing in our governmental politics can also be seen as signs of vigor and strength, while compliance and unanimity run the risk of leading to stagnation.

Most of our political leaders are what might be called "professional politicians," men and women who begin their careers in local and state politics, and rise to the national level as representatives, senators, or governors before being elected president. But America can also produce a Ronald Reagan who was a movie actor before becoming governor of California and president of the United States; an Arnold Schwarzenegger, the Austrian-born bodybuilder and movie actor also elected governor of California; and a Jesse Ventura, a professional wrestler before becoming governor of Minnesota.

CIVIL SOCIETY

Civil society commonly embraces a diversity of spaces, actors and institutional forms, varying in their degree of formality, autonomy and power. Civil societies are often populated by organisations such as registered charities, development non-governmental organisations, community groups, women's organisations, faith-based organisations, professional associations, trades unions, self-help groups, social movements, business associations, coalitions and advocacy groups.
—London School of Economics

Although there is no universally accepted definition of civil society, an anonymous scholar from the London School of Economics makes clear that it describes the part of society not under direct control of the state.

In America, however, civil society also includes a host of non-profit organizations that benefit from a provision of the Internal Revenue Code, Section 501(c)(3) that provides tax benefits for donors to such non-profits. That enables wealthy persons, as well as average individuals such as myself, to make financial contributions to groups whose objectives we share, and to get a deduction on our federal income taxes. To qualify for tax exemption an organization must be organized and operated exclusively for one or more of the purposes set forth in the tax code, and none of its earnings may inure to any private shareholder or individual. In addition, it may not attempt to influence legislation as a substantial part of its activities, and it may not in any way participate in campaign activity for or against political candidates.

Such organizations, commonly called "charitable," include, among others, religious, educational, scientific, literary, amateur sports, and the prevention of cruelty to children or animals. They also include large foundations, such as the Ford and Rockefeller foundations, as well as countless numbers of small family foundations and other organizations dedicated to particular causes.

Visitors from Europe and other parts of the world may be surprised to learn that the U.S. government has no department of culture. We do have a National Endowment for the Arts (NEA), established only in 1965, which with congressional funding makes grants in support of the arts. Its budget, however, is small, and our symphony orchestras, operas, theaters, dance companies, and others engaged in the arts must rely on support from foundations, corporations, individuals, and other non-governmental benefactors.

Why does the richest country in the world do so little in support of the arts? For that we must go back to early American history and the Puritans, the early English settlers of what are now the New England states in our northeast. The Puritans followed the Bible very closely in their effort to communicate directly with God, and to do so there had to be no distractions. To prevent distractions, the Puritans practiced an austere lifestyle. They immersed themselves in their work and avoided art, sculpture, poetry, drama or anything else that might be seen as a distraction. The result of that lifestyle of hard work was a community that was industrious, influential, and wealthy.

The long-term influence of Puritanism is still seen today throughout our country; the Puritans were among our very first settlers and they spread their ideas and values throughout the land. The Puritan work ethic became a staple of American idealism. Likewise this nation remains a Protestant country with a legacy of conservatism. The Puritans may have lasted only a little over a century, but their ideals remain.

By contrast, the arts in Europe were supported mainly by kings, local princes, and other aristocrats. When those rulers no longer ruled, it seemed perfectly logical to their former subjects that successor governments should also support the arts.

America, however, had no aristocracy and no tradition of government support for the arts. With the aggravating factor of the Puritan ethic of hard work with no distractions, the arts were slow to develop in America, and whatever support they required eventually came from non-government sources.

Education was also left to the original states because of the variety of religions and cultures in the thirteen original English colonies. There were Puritans in New England, Jews in Rhode Island and New York, Reformed Dutch in New Amsterdam (later New York), Quakers in Pennsylvania, Catholics in Maryland, and free thinkers everywhere, especially in Virginia where, in 1786, an "Act for Establishing Religious Freedom" was passed. That Act, first drafted in 1777 by Thomas Jefferson, who was to become the third president of the United States, became the model for the First Amendment to the Constitution which became law in 1791.

Volunteerism is another traditional activity that is an important part of American civil society. As de Tocqueville saw it, "The health of a democratic society may be measured by the quality of functions performed by private citizens."

In 2005, some 65 million Americans, both adults and teenagers, were engaged in some kind of volunteer service in the United States.[41] The most likely to volunteer are between the ages of 35 and 44, and more women volunteer than men. Each volunteers, on average, fifty hours of work a year. Religious organizations have the most volunteers (34.8 percent), followed closely by educational and youth services (26.2 percent).

Many Americans also volunteer for work in other countries. The best known of such organizations is the **Peace Corps**,

---

41. *Washington Post*, 13 June 2006.

which traces its roots and mission to 1960 when then-Senator John F. Kennedy challenged students at the University of Michigan to serve their country in the cause of peace by living and working in developing countries. From that inspiration grew an agency of the federal government devoted to world peace, friendship, and transfer of skills. Since that time, more than 182,000 Peace Corps volunteers have been invited by 138 host countries to work on issues ranging from HIV/AIDS education and information technology to English teaching and environmental preservation. Peace Corps volunteers generally serve for two years, and while most are in their twenties, a considerable number are over 50.

THE BUSINESS OF AMERICA

The business of America is business.
—Calvin Coolidge, 30th U.S. President

The saying, "What's good for General Motors is good for the country," and the famous quotation of Calvin Coolidge, **"The business of America is business,"** reveal the strong support Americans have for corporate America. Despite recent scandals exposing the ethical misconduct of senior executives in several major corporations, the American public is not demanding an alternative to the dominance of business. Rather than instituting radical changes, the focus is on making moderate reforms to the system.

The continued acceptance of the power and primacy of private enterprise is taken for granted by most political leaders on the left as well as the right. Moreover, Americans are also investors in their country's corporations.

Ninety-one million Americans own shares of stock directly or through mutual funds, and more than 80 million private and government workers are investors through the pension funds of their employers or their trade unions. Since American labor long ago decided that socialism was not the answer to the economic inequities of the country, it had no choice but to come to an accommodation with capitalism.

While it is not proper to ask Americans what they earn or what they are worth, some figures can provide a **benchmark** for American families. For example, the median net worth of American families in 2004 was $93,100, which means that half of all American families were worth more than that figure, and half were worth less.[42]

To do business, you need money, so it is no surprise that, in an example of American imagination and pragmatism, paper money, the dollar bill, was invented in Boston in 1691.

If you are coming to America to do business, before you sign anything, pay attention to the fine print because, as a popular saying tells us, **"the devil is in the details."** Consult a lawyer before you sign, and remember the sanctity of the contract.

---

42. Federal Reserve Survey of Consumer Finances.

THE AMERICAN DREAM

The opportunity in this country is astounding. Everyone who works hard and a little cleverly has the opportunity to make almost anything possible. That's the American Dream, that anything is possible. We are not held back. Immigrants come here, and in a single generation do extraordinary things. This country is not perfect, but compare it with every other country in the world, and it's absolutely fabulous. There's un-limited opportunity. It requires hard work, it requires a little bit of luck. But still, in America, anything is possible.
—Lawrence J. Ellison, Founder, Oracle Corporation

The American Dream is the idea, often associated with the Protestant work ethic and held by most Americans, that through hard work, courage, and determination, one can achieve prosperity. Those values were held by many of the early European settlers and have been passed on to subsequent generations.

But what the American Dream has become is a question under continuing discussion, and some believe that it has led to an overemphasis on comparative material wealth and conspicuous consumption as the major measures of success and happiness.

Success in America is often determined by the amount of

money or the quantity of material goods a person is able to accumulate. Hard work, cleverness, and persistence are valued as a means to accumulate material goods. Many see this as a way to sustain a comparatively high standard of living, but others view it as a lack of appreciation for the spiritual or human side of life.

The objective of the American Dream, as previously noted in these pages, used to be a house in the suburbs with a lawn in front, a patio in back, and a car in the garage. That goal still stands, but now it's two cars in the garage, a second one for the wife who works and brings in money so that parents can do more for their children and purchase more electronic gadgets and labor-saving devices for the home. Home ownership rates, usually high in the United States, fell during the fourth quarter of 2007 due to the collapse of the mortgage market, but nevertheless, according to the U.S. Census Bureau, home ownership still accounted for 68.9 percent of occupied homes.

WASHINGTON OR NEW YORK?

If you want a friend in Washington, get a dog.
—Harry S. Truman, 33rd U.S. President

In most countries, the largest city is the capital. The United Kingdom has London; France, Paris; Germany, Berlin; Italy, Rome; and Russia, Moscow. So why is Washington, D.C. the capital of the United States, rather than New York, and what is the difference between the two cities?

For starters, Washington is a horizontal city; spread out and with low buildings. New York is vertical, where builders had to build up because of limited land space. And Washington is green, with lots of trees; New York is concrete, with lots of hi-rise buildings. Washington is full of monuments and statues, commemorating famous figures and events in American history.

Washington was not always the capital of the United States. Both New York City and Philadelphia were once the capital, but in the year 1800, Washington became the official capital. And like much else in American politics, it was the result of a compromise reached between three of our Founding Fathers, Thomas Jefferson, Alexander Hamilton and James Madison.

In exchange for locating the new capital on the Potomac River, Madison agreed not to block legislation mandating the assumption of the states' debts by the Federal government. And so, under the plan of Pierre L'Enfant, a French-born artist and engineer who was an officer in the U.S. Army, the District of Columbia was carved out of the states of Maryland and Virginia and became the first planned city in the United States.

Despite L'Enfant's grand plan for a city of broad avenues superimposed on a grid of streets, Washington for many years was a small and sleepy town on the banks of the Potomac River with unbearable heat and humidity during the summer months. It was not until the presidency of Franklin D. Roosevelt in the 1930s, the rise in authority of the federal government, and the advent of air conditioning that Washington grew into the capital of the world power that emerged following World War II. New York meanwhile developed into the largest city of the United States and became the country's financial, commercial, and artistic center.

Which city to visit? Both, if you have the time and the money. In Washington, the Capitol and the Library of Congress are open to the public, along with some of the eighteen Smithsonian museums, several of them along the National Mall in the heart of the city, and all of them free. But Washington is not only the seat of government. The Greater Washington region is the sixth-largest regional economy in the world, bigger even than London or Seoul.

For a **birds-eye view** of the city, be sure to go to the top of the Washington Monument or the Old Post Office Building. Both are free but for the Monument, located on the Mall at 15th Street NW, you will need a ticket of admittance for a definite date and time of day. Tickets can be obtained at the base of the monument, at a kiosk on 15th Street, or by calling 1-800-967-2283. The Old Post Office Building is on Pennsylvania Avenue at 12th Street NW.

If you want to see the vibrancy of America's financial center, the skyscrapers of Manhattan, its many museums, theaters and other cultural attractions, the excitement of a big city, and a real American melting pot, be sure to visit New York City. Be prepared for the variety of people you will encounter on the sidewalks of New York—Spanish-speaking Hispanics, black Americans, Asians, colorfully-robed Africans, turbaned Sikhs, and black-clad Hassidic Jews. New York is a great walking city. Of its 8 million residents, 38 percent are foreign-born.

Despite the crowds and seeming cold nature of the city, New Yorkers can be very friendly if they recognize that you are a stranger and seem lost. Just open a street map of the city and you will be surrounded by New Yorkers eager to help, discussing and debating among themselves the best way to get you to your destination, and even offering to accompany you.

Don't fail to visit Ellis Island in New York Harbor, through which more than 22 million passengers and ships' crews passed between 1892 and 1924 on their arrival in the New World. Now a National Monument, its History of Immigration Museum tells the story of immigration to the United States. It is a rewarding experience for adults and children of all ages, and it's free, except for the ferry boat.

What Washington and New York, as well as many other large American cities, do have in common is homeless people. On any given night, reported a government survey, an estimated 754,000 people are homeless.[43] How can that be, one might ask, in the wealthiest country in the world?

There is no simple answer to the problem of the homeless. Some are free spirits who have simply withdrawn from society. Some have low-paying jobs and cannot find affordable housing, or are unemployed. Others are alcoholics or on drugs. Many others, however, are mentally ill and without treatment.

Years ago such people were placed in state mental institutions, often against their will. But with rising concern for human rights, as well as budgetary constraints, such mental institutions were phased out and responsibility was transferred to local communities. It was expected that a balance would be found between medical treatment on an out-patient basis, individual rights, and public safety, while protecting the mentally ill from wrongful commitment to mental institutions. In

---

43. *Washington Post*, 1 March 2007.

communities with sufficient resources, that has proven successful, but in others with insufficient resources it has not, and many individuals who need care but resist order and discipline in their lives have taken to the streets.

THE SMALL TOWN

Every one expects to go further than his father went; every one expects to be better than he was born and every generation has one big impulse in its heart—to exceed all the other generations of the past in all the things that make life worth living.

—William Allen White

William Allen White (1868–1944), an American journalist known as the Sage of Emporia, Kansas, symbolized much of what has been written about Americans in this book. His mixture of optimism, tolerance, liberal Republicanism and provincialism made him the epitome of the wise and witty small-town American.

Far from New York and Washington in spirit, but not necessarily distance, are the many small towns, similar to William Allen White's Emporia, that many believe represent the real America, and without which no visit to the United States is complete. There, the contrast with the big city, described earlier in these pages, will be apparent—the small town's community, friendliness, and caring for others versus the big city's individualism, self-centeredness, and alienation. In the small town, you will also find more emphasis on the family, order, stability, and nostalgia for the past, as well as conservatism in politics, as opposed to the pragmatism, openness to change, and liberalism in politics of the big city.

In the small town, the pace of life is slower, there is time for extended conversations, everyone seems to know everyone else, crime is low, hospitality is high, prices are more moderate, and visitors are welcome. Even as a complete stranger in town, you will be greeted by people on the streets.

Almost every American city and town, large or small, has a library, free and open to the public, many of them due to the beneficence of Andrew Carnegie, an immigrant from Scotland. There, you can catch up with the news of the world, read a magazine or book, access the Internet, and use the restrooms.

Carnegie, the son of a weaver, came to the United States in 1848 and began work as a bobbin boy in a cotton mill. After a succession of jobs with Western Union, a telegraph agency, and the Pennsylvania Railroad, he established his own business enterprises in 1865 and eventually organized the Carnegie Steel Company, which launched the steel industry in Pittsburgh. At age sixty-five, he sold the company for $480 million and devoted the rest of his life to philanthropic activities and writing. Similar success stories can be told for Henry Ford and John D. Rockefeller, whose descendants established foundations to aid in the improvement of the lives of so many people in America and throughout the world.

If your itinerary does not bring you near a small town, there is a Museum of Small Town Life, depicting how life used to be in small town America. Located in Dover, the state capital of Delaware, it's a short drive from Washington, D.C., and admission is free.

When You Have To "Go"

Lyndon Johnson taught me two things. He'd say never pass up a bathroom and never pass up breakfast, because you'll never know when you'll get either again.
—Bill Moyers, American journalist

Americans are proud of their indoor plumbing, but when you leave the privacy of an American hotel or home, a public toilet may be hard to find. "Toilet," moreover, seems to be a word to be avoided. The British have their "W.C." or "Loo," and the French their *toilette* and W.C. Our highways have "**Rest Stops**," and Chicagoans have their "washrooms." The most common terms, however, for American public toilets, are "**Restroom**" or "**Men's Room**" and "**Ladies Room**," although many Americans call them "**bathrooms**" despite the fact that they do not always have a tub, or "**the facilities**."

But when you "**have to go,**" as it is quaintly called, you may have difficulty finding a place to do so. Pay toilets used to be quite common, but they were outlawed a few years ago on the grounds that they discriminated against women since women need stalls whereas men do not, and because they were not accessible to the disabled.

While many major cities around the world have installed state-of-the-art public toilets which are automatically self-cleaning after each use, an American city with public toilets is still a rarity, and urinating in the streets can get you arrested by the police. So where does one "go?"

As a boy in Boston, my father told me where to go—hotels, railroad stations, and public buildings. Today you can also find restrooms accessible in fast food restaurants such as McDonald's, coffee shops such as Starbucks, large book stores like Borders or Barnes and Noble, gas stations, and supermarkets. Department stores also have them, but they are not always easy to find. One thing you can be sure of–those restrooms will be clean.

Women soon will no longer have to wait in long lines. More and more states and cities are requiring that new construction have higher ratios of women's to men's toilets. In May 2005, for example, the New York City Council unanimously approved legislation requiring public facilities to uphold a 2-to-1 ratio of women's to men's toilets.[44]

For those readers who want more information on the subject, there is a book, *Where to Stop & Where to Go: A Guide to Traveling with Overactive Bladder in the United States.* Written by the well-known travel guide writer Arthur Frommer, the brochure tells you where to find restroom locations at restaurants, museums, and other tourist attractions in nineteen U.S. cities and national parks.

Americans are very conscious of body odors and may seem to be fanatic about taking showers, washing their hair, and using many types of toiletries, such as deodorants and fragrances. As a popular saying describes it, "Cleanliness is next to godliness." Cleanliness of the home is also important, especially the bathroom. If you doubt that statement, visit any supermarket or discount store and take note of the large amount of shelf space dedicated to cleaning and personal hygiene products.

44. *Christian Science Monitor*, 19 January 2006.

MEDICAL CARE

The whole object of travel is not to set foot on foreign land;
it is at last to set foot on one's own country as a foreign land.
—G. K. Chesterton, British author

To make sure that you return home safe and sound, before you depart for America check to see if your health insurance covers you while you are in America and whether that coverage includes existing medical conditions. You may also want to purchase additional travelers' health insurance in your home country before you depart and to visit your local dentist, since dental care in America can be expensive.

U.S. hospitals are required to provide emergency care to everyone, but it will be only emergency care. After that you are on your own. You may be admitted to a hospital through its **Emergency Room** or "ER", but you most likely will be presented with a substantial bill when you are ready to leave.

If you need to find a doctor, your consulate in the United States may be helpful, and most city hospitals will be able to put you in touch with a doctor and an interpreter who speaks your language. You also have the right to ask for an interpreter in a hospital. In rural areas, county medical societies can be helpful in finding a doctor who speaks your language. Doctors are also listed by specialty in the Yellow Pages of the telephone directory.

For emergencies—to call an ambulance or the police from any-where in the United States—dial 911 on the telephone.

Visitors should be sure to carry an adequate supply of nec-essary medications because they will have difficulty getting foreign prescriptions filled here. They should also carry a list of their medications, including **over-the-counter** ones, which may require a prescription here, so that a willing American doctor can write prescriptions for them.

If you are seeking employment in the United States, make sure that medical insurance is included in your financial pack-age, and read the fine print to see what and whom it covers.

Although you may have to pay more for medical services in America, you will not have to bribe anyone to receive them. And if you or anyone in your family is hospitalized here, you won't have to provide food, blankets, clean sheets, or personal care.

EXTENDING YOUR STAY

In 2004 the United States issued 5.4 million visas, out of just more than 7 million applications. Many of those arrivals, however, wanted to extend their stay after their authorized stay had expired. Here's how to do it.

Non-immigrants wishing to extend their stay in the United States should apply at least 45 days before their authorized stay expires. However, the application must be received by a Service Center of the United States Citizenship and Immigration Services (USCIS) by the day the authorized stay expires.

If you are in any the following non-immigrant categories, you should carefully read and complete USCIS Form I-539 (Application to Extend/Change Nonimmigrant Status) and submit any required supporting documents:

A – Diplomatic and other government officials, and their families and employees

B – Temporary visitors for business or pleasure

F – Academic Students and their families

G – Representatives to international organizations and their families and employees

I – Representatives of foreign media and their families

J – Exchange Visitors and their families

M – Vocational Students and their families

N – Parents and children of the people who have been

granted special immigrant status because their parents were employed by an international organization in the United States

The application and correct fee should be mailed to the USCIS Service Center that serves the area where you are temporarily staying. If your nonimmigrant category is work-related, the application and correct fee should be mailed to the USCIS Service Center that serves the area where you will work. Forms are available by calling 1-800-870-3676, or by submitting a request through the "forms by mail" system. For further information on filing fees, see USCIS filing fees, fee waiver request procedures, and the USCIS fee waiver policy memo.[45]

Students, researchers, and professors should contact the international office at their host institution.

For other questions concerning your visa, call the toll-free number at the USCIS Customer Service Center, 1-800-375-5283.

For persons desiring to join family members in the United States, the Immigration and Nationality Act allows for the immigration of foreigners to the United States based on relationship to a U.S. citizen or legal permanent resident. Family-based immigration falls under two basic categories: unlimited and limited.

Unlimited Family-Based

Immediate Relatives of U.S. Citizens (IR): The spouse, widow(er) and unmarried children under 21 of a U.S. citizen, and the parent of a U.S. citizen who is 21 or older.

Returning Residents (SB): Immigrants who lived in the United States previously as lawful permanent residents and are returning to live in the U.S. after a temporary visit of more than one year abroad.

---

45. For more information on USCIS service centers, see USCIS field offices home pages: https://egov.uscis.gov/crisgwi/go?action=offices.type&OfficeLocator.office_type=LO

Limited Family-Based

Family First Preference (F1): Unmarried sons and daughters of U.S. citizens, and their children, if any. (23,400)

Family Second Preference (F2): Spouses, minor children, and unmarried sons and daughters (over age 20) of lawful permanent residents. (114,200) At least 77 percent of all visas available for this category will go to the spouses and children; the remainder will be allocated to unmarried sons and daughters.

Family Third Preference (F3): Married sons and daughters of U.S. citizens, and their spouses and children. (23,400)

Family Fourth Preference (F4): Brothers and sisters of United States citizens, and their spouses and children, provided the U.S. citizens are at least 21 years of age. (65,000)

It may seem complicated but U.S. government officials are there to help, and they are only a telephone call away.

POSTSCRIPT

Our "snapshot" tour of America is now completed. You have read about the pluses and the minuses, the do's and the don'ts, the good and the not so good. The rest, dear visitor, is up to you. Travel widely, meet lots of people, and make up your own mind about America. And enjoy your visit.

Appendix A
Glossary of Useful Words and Idioms

Aka A short term for "also known as."

All men are created equal. One of the most famous phrases found in American political documents, it was originally suggested by Italian immigrant Phillip Mazzei and incorporated by Thomas Jefferson in the Declaration of Independence as "We hold these truths to be self-evident, that all men are created equal, that they are endowed by their Creator with certain unalienable Rights, that among these are Life, Liberty and the pursuit of Happiness."

All you can eat Also known as "buffets," this is special option found in some restaurants where patrons serve themselves from long buffet tables of food and can eat all they want for a fixed price.

American Civil Liberties Union (ACLU) A non-governmental organization established to defend and preserve the individual rights and liberties guaranteed to every person in the country by the Constitution and laws of the United States. Causes that the ACLU is most known for advocating include free speech, privacy, and freedom of information (about the government).

Alma Mater From the latin for "foster mother," a term used to describe a person's school or college.

American dream The hope for a successful and happy life.

babysitter Someone who is hired to care for children when their parents are away.

bathroom A room in a home that contains a sink, toilet, and perhaps a bath.

Beat around the bush To talk around a subject, rather than address it directly.

benchmark A standard used to measure or judge something

Best is yet to come. Things will be better in the future, an expression of American optimism.

best-seller A book, popular with the public, and included in a list of best-selling books.

Big Apple A common and affectionate nickname for New York City.

Big Brother A pejorative reference to a totalitarian government or system that suppress individual freedoms and rights under the guise of protecting and caring for those individuals.

big ticket A high-priced item.

Bill of Rights The first ten amendments to the Constitution of the United States which protect the rights of citizens.

birds-eye view A panoramic view from a high point.

Blow your own horn. To promote yourself to others.

Bon appétit. French for wishing someone a "good appetite."

bone-cruncher A too-firm handshake that could hurt the hand being shaken.

Born-again Christian A person who has made a conversion to, or renewed his or her commitment to, Jesus Christ as personal savior.

brain-storming A method of problem solving in which members of a group spontaneously propose ideas that have occurred to them, whether practical or not.

brass tacks The main points in any discussion (see also "Getting down to brass tacks").

brunch A leisurely late morning meal that combines breakfast and lunch. Usually enjoyed by Americans on weekends, particularly after Sunday religious ceremonies.

campus The grounds and buildings of a college or university, often a town unto itself.

Can do. An expression of American optimism and willingness to take on a task and get it done.

car pool A group of people who drive to work in one car.

Casual Friday A policy or understanding maintained in some companies that allows employees to come to work on Fridays wearing casual clothing.

catch-as-catch-can Using whatever is available.

charter schools Public non-sectarian schools, funded by local government and open to all, but operated independently under a charter that makes them accountable for results.

checks and balances A feature of the U.S. Constitution whereby each of the three branches of government–executive, legislative, and judicial–are expected to limit the power of the others and prevent any of them from becoming too powerful.

Civil Society The voluntary and other non-governmental organizations and institutions that form the basis of a functioning society.

civil union A legally recognized union of two people, similar to marriage, performed by a government official and that provides same sex couples with rights, benefits, and responsibilities similar to those of opposite-sex couples. These unions are politically controversial, as many consider them to be a form of discrimination against homosexual couples.

classic A book, film, or other work of art believed to have lasting appeal.

couch potato A person who is considered to spend too much time sitting or lying down, and usually watching television or playing video games.

designated driver One who agrees to stay sober at a party in order to drive the others safely home.

DJ (Disc Jockey) An announcer, usually on radio, who presents and comments on recorded music.

doggie bag A bag or box of uneaten food ("leftovers") to take home from a restaurant.

Don't just stand there, do something! Take action, don't just be an observer.

downside A disadvantage.

dress down To wear informal clothes.

Drop by some time. A colloquialism meaning "stop in for a short visit."

Dutch treat A meal (or other event) where each person attending pays his/her expenses (occasionally, in large groups and at restaurants, the bill will simply be split evening among the attendees, with each paying an equal portion).

DUI Driving under the influence of alcohol or drugs. A criminal offense.

DWI Driving while intoxicated. A criminal offense, even more serious than a DUI.

E pluribus unum. A Latin phrase meaning "One from many" and found on U.S. currency.

The early bird catches the worm. Don't delay taking action.

Emergency Room A part of a hospital that treats emergency cases, also called "the E.R."

Excuse me. Used to acknowledge or ask forgiveness for something that could offend (such as bumping a person on the street) or to politely attract the attention of a stranger.

Executive Branch The departments and agencies of the federal government, headed by the President.

extracurricular activities Activities outside work or formal courses of instruction.

facilities A restroom.

fairness Impartiality, free of favoritism or undue advantages.

Founding Fathers Leaders of the American Revolution and movement for independence from England.

gas guzzler A large vehicle that consumes too much gasoline.

Getting ahead Winning, or in advance of a competitor. Also may refer to having increasing success in life.

Getting down to brass tacks Skipping the introductory small talk and instead discussing the important things.

God helps those who help themselves. God will help us only if we first try to help ourselves.

going Dutch A group goes out to eat, and each person pays for his/her own food (or each pays an equal portion of the bill).

good sport One who accepts defeat without complaint.

Grease someone's palm Pay a bribe.

happy ending A satisfactory conclusion to a movie, novel, or events in real life.

hardheaded Stubborn.

hard liquor A beverage with high alcoholic content, like whiskey, vodka, gin, cognac.

have to go Need to urinate or defecate.

He who hesitates is lost. Don't delay taking action.

Hit a home run Baseball expression, indicating complete success.

hitchhike To seek free transportation from strangers by standing at the side of the road, arm extended and thumb pointing in the direction you are going. Though very common in America prior to the 1980s, hitchhiking is now illegal in most states, for safety considerations.

House of Representatives The lower body of the U.S. Congress, consisting of 435 members who serve 2-year terms and represent the people of the 50 states according to population.

I don't care how you get it done—just do it! The result is more important than the method.

In Search Of Advertisement in newspaper or magazine for people looking to meet others of the opposite or same sex, usually for the purpose of dating.

It will work out. Everything will be okay in the long run.

jaywalking Crossing a street at an unauthorized place.

Judicial Branch The court system of the federal government, headed by the U.S. Supreme Court.

Keeping up with the Joneses To match or equal the lifestyle of one's neighbors. Also refers to the culture of consumerism in America.

kosher Conforming to Jewish dietary laws.

Ladies' Room Restroom for women.

larger than life Very impressive.

left field Far from the conventional wisdom.

Legislative Branch The U.S. Congrress, consisting of the Senate and House of Representative, which legislates the laws of the land.

leisure activities Activities performed in free time, such as reading.

Let's get together sometime. Invite to meet again but not set a firm date or time.

level playing field Conditions equal for both sides in a competition.

linkage In negotiating, making one step or point dependent on another.

litigious From "litigate," to engage in lawsuits.

lone cowboy One who tends to live a solitary lifestyle, or tackle issues alone.

McMansion A very large house built in a neighborhood of smaller houses.

meet halfway and make a deal To compromise, especially where each side gets something it wants.

melting pot Immigrants with different cultures coming together to make a new society.

Men's Room Restroom for men.

middle-of-the-road position A position halfway between two extremes.

moving the goalposts Adding an additional task to overcome.

My country, right or wrong. Unquestioning patriotism—to support one's country, whether it is in the right or wrong.

my ex A person's former wife or husband.

Nation of laws, not men Laws, not men, determine how a country should be run.

National Guard Reserve military units, equipped by the federal government but under the command of each state, and subject to call-up by the state or federal government.

Native Americans A member of any of the indigenous peoples of the Western Hemisphere, formerly known incorrectly as Indians.

Never put off until tomorrow what you can do today. Don't delay taking action.

No-fault divorce Divorce in which neither spouse is required to prove 'fault' or marital misconduct on the part of the other.

no-no Something strictly forbidden.

nose to the grindstone Working hard and steadily.

Old Country For immigrants, their country of origin.

Old-fashioned An older style (of thinking, clothing, decoration, etc.) that is no longer popular.

on the one-yard line U.S. football term, indicating one is close to victory.

out-patient A patient treated outside a hospital.

outsider One who is not part of an organization or movement.

Opportunity knocks only once. You may not have a second chance to do something.

partner One united with another in a common activity; also a person sharing a domicile with another, of the same or opposite sex.

Peace Corps An agency of the U.S. Government which sends volunteers abroad to help developing countries meet their need for trained men and women.

pecking order A ranking of superiority, usually among people.

Personals Advertisement in newspaper or magazine for people looking to meet people of the opposite or same sex.

Political Correctness (PC) Makes it incorrect to use pejorative terms or stereotypes to describe or talk about people's gender, race, sexuality, or creed.

potluck A type of dinner party where each guest brings a dish for the group to eat.

potty parity A movement to require all new or remodeled sports or entertainment facilities to be equipped with a minimum number of toilets for women and men.

poverty line A level of income, set by the government, below which a person is officially seen to be living in poverty.

pre-nup An agreement prior to marriage (nuptial) specifying which assets will remain the property of the future wife or husband.

privacy The ability of an individual or group to control the release and obtaining of information about themselves. Also, the (limited) right to be left alone by government.

Protestant work ethic Calvinist value emphasizing labor as a sign of personal salvation.

PTA Parent-Teacher Association, a non-profit organization of parents and teachers that supports a local school.

public schools U.S primary and secondary schools which are supported by public funds, and are free and open to all children.

private school Schools supported by private funding, often religiously affiliated.

The proof of the pudding is in the eating. The result is more important than the process.

Put the ball in the other guy's court. Tennis expression indicating that your opponent must make the next move.

rags to riches From poverty to wealth—the American success story.

raincheck Postponing something until another day.

report card A periodic report issue by school that outlines on each student's progress, to be read and signed by a parent, and returned to the school.

results driven Judgment of value of something according to the results produced.

restroom Room equipped with toilets in a public building.

rest stop Area along a public highway equipped with toilets, highway maps, picnic tables and, occasionally, food and beverage vending machines.

road rage Violent, irrational anger shown by drivers in traffic.

roadside assistance Mechanical assistance for cars broken down on highways, usually provided free under certain kinds of insurance coverage.

rugged individualist Complimentary description for a person who succeeds without help from others.

rule of thumb A customary practice, but not necessarily applicable in every case.

rush hour Periods in the morning and early evening when roads are jammed with commuters.

salad bar A restaurant or a section of a restaurant where you can serve yourself with fresh vegetables and salads, and pay only for what you take or according to a fixed price.

safe sex The use of condoms and other precautionary procedures during sex, with the aim of preventing the spread of sexually transmitted diseases or unwanted pregnancies.

self-made man One who achieves success without help from others.

Senate The upper body of the U.S. Congress whose 100 members, two for each state, serve for 6-year terms.

senior citizen Person of advanced age, usually retired.

separate but equal Slogan used in the past to justify separate schools for blacks.

sex appeal Characteristics that attract others sexually.

shortcut A more direct approach to doing something, in order to save time.

shoulder to the wheel Applying yourself seriously to a task.

siding with the underdog Supporting the weaker and less favored person in a competition.

significant other Spouse or partner with whom one shares a sexual relationship.

slang Common language uage.

small talk Casual and unimportant conversation.

soccer mom Mother in a U.S. community who spends much time driving children to and from athletic or other events.

soft drinks Non-alcoholic drinks, usually flavored and carbonated, and sold in bottles or cans.

Special Education Classroom or private instruction designed for students with a disability whose learning needs cannot be met by a standard school curriculum.

speed bump A low ridge installed across a road to make drivers reduce speed.

Stand on ceremony Observe traditional customs or rules in performing an action.

Stand on your own two feet Perform an action by yourself without help from others.

sticker price The announced or advertised sales price.

stats Short form of "statistics."

stiff upper lip Determined durability in the face of adversity.

strike out Baseball term signifying failure.

Strike while the iron is hot. Don't delay taking action.

stuffed shirt Pompous or stiff person, impressed with own importance.

suburb A region around a big city where people live and commute to work in the city.

Sue me. Challenge indicating you believe you are right—and not going to change your position.

Supreme Court The highest court of the land, consisting of 9 justices, appointed by the President and confirmed by the Senate, and who serve as long as they are able.

sweet tooth Craving for sweets.

swing vote In U.S. politics, the undecided block of voters that could potentially be won by either major political party.

tailgate The rear door of a station wagon which, when opened, can serve as a table.

teetotaler One who does not drink alcoholic beverages.

Tell it like it is. Be realistic, even if the truth may hurt you or the feelings of others.

Thanksgiving Day The fourth Thursday in November, a national holiday commemorating the feast held in 1621 by the Pilgrims to thank God for a successful first harvest.

There are many ways to skin a cat. The result is more important than the method.

Three Rs—reading, writing, and 'rithmetic A popular saying, once considered the basics of schooling.

Time is money. Indicating that there is a real cost to time, and it should not be wasted.

tip A helpful suggestion. Also, the gratuity you leave for a waiter or other person who has been helpful.

try harder Slogan indicating striving for excellence.

Up-scale Expensive and intended for high-income people.

vegan A vegetarian who further refrains from eating any animal byproducts, including eggs or dairy.

volunteerism Use of unpaid volunteers to perform needed services.

War between the States U.S. Civil War, 1861–1865.

warehouse To treat people as if they were a commodity to be stored in a warehouse.

wasband A former husband.

win-win Solution to a conflict or disagreement where both sides gain something they want.

women's lib Movement to achieve equal rights for women.

Women's Room Lavatory, with toilets, for women.

Yellow Pages Listings in a local telephone directory for business telephone numbers, organized by business type.

You made your own bed, now lie in it. Be responsible for your own actions.

zebra crossing White stripes on the street pavement, indicating authorized crossing points for pedestrians.

Appendix B
National Holidays

The United States has ten federal holidays set by law, when all government offices, and most businesses and private institutions, are closed. Four holidays are set by date:

New Year's Day	January 1
Independence Day	July 4
Veterans' Day	November 11
Christmas Day	December 25

If any of the above fall on a Saturday, then Friday may be observed as a holiday by various institutions. Similarly, if one falls on a Sunday, then Monday may be observed as a holiday. The other six are set by a day of the week in a certain month:

Martin Luther King's Birthday	Third Monday in January
President's Day	Third Monday in February
Memorial Day	Last Monday in May
Labor Day	First Monday in September
Columbus Day	Second Monday in October
Thanksgiving	Fourth Thursday in November

As you can see, Americans like their holidays on Mondays because it gives them a long weekend.

Resources

U.S. Citizenship and Immigration Services (USCIS) (for visa questions): Toll-free Tel. 1-800-375-5283

Institute of International Education (IIE), 809 United Nations Plaza, 7th Floor, New York, NY, 10017, Tel. (212) 984-5370

Council for International Exchange of Scholars (Fulbright Scholar Program), 3007 Tilden St., NW, Washington, DC, 20008. Tel. (202) 686-4000.

National Council for International Visitors (NCIV), 1420 K St., NW, Suite 800, Washington, DC 20005-2401 Tel. (202) 842-1414, http://www.nciv.org.

152

RECOMMENDED READINGS

Bryson, Bill. *I'm a Stranger Here Myself: Notes on Returning to America After Twenty Years Away.* New York: Broadway Books, 1999.

Lévy, Bernard-Henri. *Atlantic*, May, June, July. "In the Footsteps of Tocqueville."

Lévy, Bernard-Henri. *American Vertigo: Traveling America in the Footsteps of Tocqueville.* New York: Random House, 2005.

MacNeil, Robert and William Cran. *Do You Speak American?* New York: Harcourt Trade Publishers, 2005.

Quinney, Nigel. "U.S. Negotiating Behavior," Special Report 94. Washington, DC: U.S. Institute of Peace, October 2002. http://www.usip.org/pubs/specialreports/sr94.html

Tocqueville, Alexis de. *Democracy in America.* Library of America, 2004.

Wederspahn, Gary. *A Worldwide Buyer's Guide and Sourcebook.* Oxford: Butterworth Heinemann, 2000.

America is so vast that almost everything said about it is likely to be true, and the opposite is probably equally true.
—James T. Farrell, American writer

Other Travel and History Titles from Hippocrene Books

The Navajo Nation: A Visitor's Guide
Patrick and Joan Lavin

This unique guidebook opens with a section on the history of the Navajo from pre-colonial times to the present, with a special focus on the development of their culture and religion. The next section is a comprehensive visitor's guide to the region, covering sites of historical interest and natural beauty and including driving directions, accommodations, and other helpful information. Finally, a section on the Navajo language gives readers a flavor for speaking Navajo and includes useful words and phrases.

283 pages · 5½ x 8½ · 0-7818-1180-5 · $21.95pb

Long Island: A Guide to New York's Suffolk and Nassau Counties
Raymond Edward Spinzia, Judith Ader Spinzia and Kathryn Spinzia Rayne

Known for its beautiful beaches, fishing villages, quaint towns, and world-famous wineries, Long island welcomes thousands of visitors every year. Here is a completely revised and updated edition of the first comprehensive guidebook to Long Island's Suffolk and Nassau counties. Organized by town and then subdivided into the various villages and hamlets, this popular guide provides entries for each locale. This book includes directions from the Long Island Expressway to places of special interest: federal, state, and county parks and preservers; museums; historical sites and much more.

269 pages · 6 x 9 · 0-7818-1213-9 · $24.95pb

Intelligence Was My Line: Inside Eisenhower's Other Command
182 pages · 5½ x 8½ · 0-7818-1117-1 · $24.95pb

Voices of American Muslims
279 pages · 6 x 9 · 0-7818-1039-6 · $14.95pb

Gettysburg: Crisis of Command
297 pages · 5½ x 8½ · 0-7818-1039-6 · $14.95pb

Illustrated History Titles from Hippocrene Books

New Mexico: An Illustrated History
Patrick Lavin

Known as the "Land of Enchantment," New Mexico is living witness to the coexistence of Native American, Spanish, and Anglo civilizations. In this book, Patrick Lavin takes an all-inclusive approach to New Mexico's past by vividly reconstructing the state's key historical events in a concise and accessible format. With more than 50 illustrations, photographs, and maps, this title provides a thorough and lively historical overview that reveals the heart and soul of this fascinating southwestern state. Citing fascinating material from newspapers, journals, and personal accounts of pioneers and explorers, this compelling volume relates the arrival of the Paleo-Indians, Spanish exploration and colonization, the Mexican-American War and subsequent territorial period, as well as New Mexico's early statehood and the post-World War II era. Today, New Mexico continues to inspire visitors and artists who come to pay tribute to the state's magnificent natural beauty and cultural heritage.

253 pages · 5½ x 8½ · 0-7818-1053-1 · $14.95pb

Pennsylvania: An Illustrated History
Donald E. Markle

Originally settled by Swedes, Pennsylvania became the single largest land grant to an individual in history when Charles II of England signed it over to William Penn in 1681. As a result, the colony evolved into a core of American politics, culture and social reform. This concise volume opens with the history of Pennsylvania from the Native American era to colonial times, when Philadelphia serves as the birthplace and first capital of a new nation. It then progresses through the centuries to explore the iron, steel, coal and oil industries that developed in the nineteenth century. It concludes with a look at modern-day Pennsylvania's complex economy and workforce. With 50 black and white photos, illustrations and maps, this book gives you an extensive look into the background and history of Pennsylvania.

269 pages · 5½ x 8½ · 0-7818-1197-2 · $14.95pb

Arizona: An Illustrated History
225 pages · 5 x 7 · 0-7818-0582-9· $14.95pb

California: An Illustrated History
252 pages · 5½ x 8½ · 0-7818-1034-5· $14.95pb

Missouri: An Illustrated History
269 pages · 5½ x 8½ · 0-7818-1196-1 · $14.95pb

Florida: An Illustrated History
238 pages · 5½ x 8½ · 0-7818-1052-3 · $14.95pb

Virginia: An Illustrated History
220 pages · 5½ x 8½ · 0-7818-1115-5 · $14.95pb

Arab World: An Illustrated History
293 pages · 5½ x 8½ · 0-7818-0990-8 · $14.95pb

Byzantium: An Illustrated History
254 pages · 5½ x 8½ · 0-7818-1033-7 · $14.95pb

London: An Illustrated History
256 pages · 5 x 7 · 0-7818-0908-8 · $14.95pb

Paris: An Illustrated History
182 pages · 5½ x 8½ · 0-7818-0838-3 · $12.95pb

Egypt: An Illustrated History
160 pages · 5 x 7 · 0-7818-1034-5 · $12.95pb

England: An Illustrated History
252 pages · 5½ x 8½ · 0-7818-1034-5 · $14.95pb

France: An Illustrated History
214 pages · 5 x 7 · 978-0-7818-1034-5 · $14.95pb

India: An Illustrated History
234 pages · 5 x 6½ · 0-7818-0944-4 · $14.95pb

Italy: An Illustrated History
142 pages · 5 x 7 · 0-7818-0819-7 · $14.95pb

Korea: An Illustrated History from Ancient Times to 1945
147 pages · 5 x 7 · 0-7818-0873-1 · $12.95pb

Poland: An Illustrated History, color edition
252 pages · 5½ x 8½ · 978-0-7818-1200-9 · $19.95pb

Romania: An Illustrated History
298 pages · 5 x 7 · 0-7818-0935-5 · $14.95pb

Sicily: An Illustrated History
152 pages · 5 x 7 · 0-7818-0909-6 · $12.95pb

Spain: An Illustrated History
175 pages · 5 x 7 · 0-7818-0874-X · $12.95pb